SPIRITUALLY CORRECT
CORRECT
Favorites

SPIRITUALLY CORRECT
Favorites

Three Bestselling Works Complete In One Volume

Spiritually Correct Bedtime Stories

The 77 Habits of Highly Ineffective Christians

Away with the Manger

CHRIS FABRY

Previously published in three separate volumes:

SPIRITUALLY CORRECT BEDTIME STORIES
Copyright © 1995 by Christopher H. Fabry.
Illuminated letters: Don Frye

77 HABITS OF HIGHLY INEFFECTIVE CHRISTIANS
Copyright © 1997 by Christopher H. Fabry.

AWAY WITH THE MANGER
Copyright © 1996 by Christopher H. Fabry.
Illuminated letters: Don Frye

First Inspirational Press edition published in 1999.

Inspirational Press
A division of BBS Publishing Corporation
386 Park Avenue South
New York, NY 10016

Inspirational Press is a registered trademark of BBS Publishing Corporation.

Published by arrangement with InterVarsity Press.

Library of Congress Catalog Card Number: 99-71870

ISBN: 0-88486-251-8

Printed in the United States of America.

Contents

SPIRITUALLY CORRECT
BEDTIME STORIES

Parables of Faith For
The Modern Reader

*For my mother, who read to me
and gave the gift of laughter,
and for all who do the same.*

INTRODUCTION

If you're in the mood to look in the mirror and laugh, you've picked up the right book. Somewhere between puberty and the first mortgage we tend to lose that ability to smile at ourselves. I'm not sure why. Maybe we need a bigger mirror.

People of faith are particularly wary of too much laughing, often because we think it's childish. Of course there's quite a difference between being child*ish* and being child*like*. It's childish to whine when you don't get your way or fret about things you have no control over. But it is childlike to laugh from your toes. It's childlike to trust so much that you slip your hand into your father's and skip down the sidewalk. These stories should be taken in with such wonder.

Some will no doubt read too much into them or try to read between the lines. Please resist the urge. Have fun. Skip through the pages like a child.

If you do happen to come away with a deep, life-changing truth, I will rejoice. I'll also be happy to hear that you stopped several times because your blood pressure rises when you chuckle. I'm sure there's medication for that.

For those who simply must know where I'm coming from, I own several study Bibles, we've educated our kids at home and in public schools, I vote regularly and think we should be involved in the political process, I love Christian publishers, I believe prophecy and angels are important for biblical study, I support seeker and traditional churches alike, I love traditional hymns and praise choruses, and I know many who have found personal comfort and help from Christian psychologists.

What you see reflected in these tales are extremes. It's a broad-brush view of the issues and movements we find in Christian circles today.

There is a Latin phrase that beautifully sums up what I want you to learn from these tales. Unfortunately I didn't do well in Latin, and I won't ask someone who did because I'm an American male. I think it's something like *Carpe Smilem,* but I'll probably never know for sure. Sorry. Enjoy them anyway.

THE THREE
THEOLOGICAL PIGS

nce upon a time there were three pigs who lived in a house with their devout mother.

One day she said to her children, "You have learned all you can from Sunday school. It is time you went on for deeper study." So the three pigs packed their bags and applied to a fine seminary. Alas, only one pig was actually accepted, so the other two settled for a correspondence course.

After a time, the three pigs started their ministries. The first met a man with a load of straw theology. "Please, sir," he said, "will you give me some to build my church?"

"Certainly," said the man, and he also gave the pig a sign that said, "Miracles Galore Tonight."

Quick as a wink the first pig's church went up, and a large congregation was attracted to each service. The little pig promised healing, prosperity and more pleasing snouts for everyone. Little did he know it was the big, bad wolf who had actually given him the straw. The wolf lurked in the narthex, watching the pig's success.

The little pig was about to start an "Oinking in the Spirit" service when he heard a knock on his study door.

"Little pig, little pig, let me in," said the wolf. "I want to contribute to the building program."

"Well, come right in," said the little pig. But when he saw it was a wolf he turned his curly tail, splashed through the baptistery and headed for his brother's church.

Meanwhile, the second pig had met a man who was carrying a load of sticks. This of course was also the wolf, who had many disguises and more building materials than you could—yes, shake a stick at.

"Please, sir," said the little pig, "will you give me some of that kindling to build my church?"

The wolf agreed and gave suggestions to the little pig for a really big turnout at Sunday's praise service.

As quick as two winks, the second pig built his church, complete with a massive parking lot. Then he built an Olympic-sized swimming pool, an ice rink, basketball courts and a sanctuary with stained glass, and he thanked his Creator for allowing him to do it all on credit. He was in one of the community rooms leading a "Swines Anonymous" twelve-step program when his brother came bursting through the door.

"You've got to help me!" the first little pig exclaimed.

"Sit down," said his brother, "and we'll help you deal with your pain."

"You don't understand. There's a big, bad wolf chasing me, and he's coming this way."

"I'm glad you're facing your fears," said the brother. "The first step is always admitting you have a problem."

Suddenly they heard a knock at the door.

"Don't let him fool you with the building program line," said the first little pig.

"Who is it?" called the brother.

"Little pigs, let me in," said the wolf. "I'm in need of counseling."

The brother immediately opened the door and gave the wolf his hourly rate.

"Silly pig," the wolf growled, "the only counseling I'll need is Overeaters Anonymous, because I'm going to gobble up you both."

The wolf did just that and felt very proud of the accomplishment. Then, since wolves are not at all shame-based, he picked himself up and headed over to eat the third pig.

When he got there, he peeked into an old shack and saw the pig kneeling. The pig was gaunt from hunger, for he had been fasting. Furthermore, the little pig had spent many years and much money in seminary and had only a tiny bit of money for food.

Feeling quite full, the wolf sat down outside the window and listened.

"And please," the pig prayed, "please keep the few pigs we have in the congregation unspotted from the world, and keep me true to my first love."

Wearying of the pig's prayers, the wolf set out to eat him, bony as he was. He tapped lightly on the door and whispered, "Little pig, little pig, where is your church building, and what time are your Sunday services?"

The little pig stopped praying and said, "We have no building, friend. We meet in the wee schoolhouse on the corner and can afford only an eleven-o'clock worship."

"If you'll come out," said the crafty wolf, "I will contribute enough for two buildings."

"It is written," the little pig said: "'Why should I fear when wicked deceivers surround me—those who trust in their wealth and boast of their great riches?'"

"And who are you to touch one anointed from on high?" scoffed the wolf. "Open the door and you will see how much I can bless you."

Because of his discerning spirit, the little pig refused to accept the wolf's invitation.

Filled with rage, the wolf yelled, "Little pig, let me in, or I'll huff and I'll puff and I'll blow holes in your theology!"

" 'The grass withers and the flowers fall, but the word of the Lord stands forever.' "

The wolf tried to climb into the shack through the window, but he slipped and fell, and his bulging stomach burst and the two little pigs popped out.

"Thank you, brother," said the pigs.

"I've been praying you would visit our church someday," said the third pig, "but I never thought you'd arrive like this!"

And the pigs talked and wept, repented and forgave, and prayed together. To this day they are ministering mightily in a very small congregation upwind of the sty.

THE THREE HOLY
GOATS GRUFF

igh on a lush hillside in a deep green pasture there lived three Holy Goats Gruff. They spent their days in harmony and fellowship, having potluck praise-and-prayer suppers and enjoying creation.

At the foot of the hill lay a wide, deep stream and a bridge they had not crossed in many years. Underneath the bridge lived a horrible, mean, nasty, worldly troll who, as it was told in those parts, was a card-carrying member of several liberal organizations. He referred to the goats as "those fundamentalists" and was bent on keeping the holy goats separated from society.

On the other side of the stream was a rocky slope covered with dangerous crags. The forlorn animals that stumbled about on these rocks did not enjoy creation like the Holy Goats Gruff did, because they did not know their Creator.

The Holy Goats Gruff were so busy with dinners and the fun they were having that they didn't think about the other side of the stream. They were content with their little slice of heavenly pasture.

But one day the littlest Holy Goat Gruff, who had a particularly sensitive conscience, spoke up. "This morning I was thinking about the good things we enjoy every day and how lighthearted we are with the bounty we possess," he said. "But when I looked on the other side of the stream I saw despondent and dejected animals. I believe we need to cross the bridge and tell others what we have found."

"What about the horrible, mean, card-carrying troll?" the Middle Holy Goat Gruff said.

"We'll invite him too," the Little Holy Goat Gruff said innocently.

"We're behind you," the Big Holy Goat Gruff said. "Lead the way."

Little Holy Goat Gruff went trip-trapping across the bridge with his little hoofs.

"Who's making that confounded noise on my bridge?" said the troll, exiting his computer's liberal on-line forum.

"It is I, Little Holy Goat Gruff," said the goat in his wee small voice. "I have come to help restore a sense of morality in a society plagued with ills. I have chosen the political arena to make a difference."

"Oh no you're not," roared the troll. "I am coming up to eat you!"

Little Holy Goat Gruff was afraid. "Oh, please don't eat me," he said. "Wait for my big brother. He is much more conservative and is much larger and tastier than I am. Anyway, what can a little goat like me do in such a world as this?"

"Good point," the troll said, licking his lips. "I wouldn't want to waste my appetite on a scrawny kid like you. Besides, you're too young to vote. Go ahead and cross."

So Little Holy Goat Gruff crossed the bridge safely and engaged the culture on the other side.

Then Middle Holy Goat Gruff's middle-sized hoofs came clomping across the wooden bridge.

"Who's that clomping over my bridge?" called the troll.

"It is I, Middle Holy Goat Gruff," said the goat in his middle-sized voice.

"Don't you know there's a separation between church and state?" the troll roared. "I am coming up to eat you!"

Middle Holy Goat Gruff was afraid and thought about turning back. But he saw his younger brother encouraging him from the other side, so he stood his ground.

"I have a right to go on that side of the stream like anyone else," he said. "I am going into education to touch lives by teaching truth to young minds."

"No you aren't!" screamed the troll. "We can't have your kind imposing your morality and inflicting your values on our children! You'll think you have a right to sit on the school board. I'm going to start gobbling if you don't scram."

Middle Holy Goat Gruff shook with fear and said, "Please don't eat me. Wait for my big brother. He is tastier, much more conservative, and has a Rush Limbaugh figure."

"Hmmm," said the troll, "that *would* be a good meal. I don't want to spoil my appetite on you. Just make sure you don't use the word *God* or bring a Bible to class. That really gets my goat."

So Middle Holy Goat Gruff crossed the bridge safely and secured a teaching position at the local high school on the other side.

Then Big Holy Goat Gruff stepped onto the bridge. Its planks sagged under his weight, and with each hoofstep the whole bridge shook.

"Who is that sagging the planks on my bridge?" roared the troll in his loudest voice.

"It is I, Big Holy Goat Gruff," the goat shouted.

"I suppose you're going to tell me to wait for your big brother," said the troll.

"No, I am the biggest one there is," said Big Holy Goat Gruff. "I am on my way to law school to right injustice and learn how to write a friend-of-the-court brief."

"Oh no you're not!" bellowed the troll. "You have no right meddling in laws on this side of the stream.

Go back to your lush hillside, or I'll come up to eat you!"

"Come on up," said Big Holy Goat Gruff. "I am ready to meet you."

The troll climbed onto the bridge and rushed at Big Holy Goat Gruff. To his surprise the goat was sitting on the bridge looking very placid.

"What in the world are you doing?" roared the troll.

"I am staging a nonviolent protest against your anti-free-speech bullying," said Big Holy Goat Gruff.

Standing beside the goat was a man who produced a piece of paper. "I am legal counsel for the three clients known as H. G. Gruff," said this man, a lawyer from Concerned Mammals of America. "This is a restraining order for you to cease and desist your unlawful actions against them."

The troll was so angry that he sent several press releases to his colleagues in the media, but to no avail. Finally he jumped into the icy waters and disappeared beneath the flood.

After that the three Holy Goats Gruff crossed the bridge whenever they liked and brought many fellow animals over to the lush green hillside. They remained true to their convictions of restoring virtue and values to the land and were good examples to everyone.

The horrible mean troll resurfaced downstream and started a lobby against the goats and their kind. But to this day the Holy Goats Gruff remain steadfast in their pursuit of justice, and they pray daily that the troll will turn from his ways and join them in the quiet pasture.

CHICKEN LITTLE

hicken Little was picking up corn in the barnyard one bright sunny day. The wind ruffled her feathers and turned the pages of the magazine she was reading, *Today's Christian Chicken*. Suddenly, an object fell from above and clunked her on the head.

Chicken Little dropped her corn and magazine and looked up. She could see trees swaying, and it seemed to her the sky was falling.

Then she looked behind her and saw the object, a long piece of folded paper. "Dear me," she clucked. "I wonder what it is."

Soon she discovered she was holding a copy of a new bill to be passed in Congress that very day.

Though it seemed innocent, it had an obscure provision that left the door open for barn-based health clinics.

"Oh my," she clucked. "This is worse than the sky falling."

As Chicken Little ran past the big red barn, she met her friend Henny Penny, who was watching over the church day-care center.

"Why, Chicken Little, where are you going in such a hurry?" cackled Henny Penny.

"Oh dear, haven't you heard about the new bill? It will bring a new agenda to the barnyard. I am going to complain to the king!"

"Oh, Chicken Little, how do you know that?" asked Henny Penny.

"I saw it and I read it and I've been afraid this would happen all along!" clucked Chicken Little.

"I'll come with you, Chicken Little," cackled Henny Penny, and she put a *McChick and Me* video in the VCR and left her class peeping happily.

They ran past the barn and various pieces of farm machinery. Soon they met Cocky Locky, who was forever preening himself for his spiritual accomplishments.

"Well, where are you two going in such a hurry?" cackled Cocky Locky.

"Oh dear, today Congress is voting on a new bill that will surely change the farm. I think it will ban all religious speech or something, and we are going to complain to the king," said Henny Penny.

"How do you know that?" asked Cocky Locky in wonderment.

"Chicken Little told me!"

"Then let's catch up with her and tell the king!" crowed Cocky Locky. "I have a personal friend in the cabinet."

Soon they came to the edge of the pond. There was Groggy Froggy sunning himself in the mud. "Hello," he said. "Why are you running so fast on such a warm day?"

"Oh dear, Groggy Froggy, a new bill in Congress will ban anything Christian in print, on television, on radio and even in our church, so we're going to tell the king!" Cocky Locky crowed. "You know how successful I've been at defeating the liberal lobby."

"But how do you know there's such a bill?" ribbeted Groggy Froggy.

Cocky Locky said, "Henny Penny told me."

Henny Penny said, "Chicken Little told me."

"My, my," said Groggy Froggy as he jumped from his bed of mud. "Wait for me. I'll come too." And he hopped along after them.

At the other end of the pond, Lucille Goose (who did not like to be called "Loosey") was teaching her goslings to honk in tongues. She looked up and saw the animals running down the lane.

"Where are you going?" she said.

"Oh dear, a bill is passing," ribbeted Groggy Froggy importantly, "and it will take away our belief in God, and we're going to complain to the king."

"But who told you that a bill is passing?" asked Lucille.

"Cocky Locky told me," said Groggy Froggy.

"Henny Penny told me," said Cocky Locky.

"Chicken Little told me!" said Henny Penny.

Chicken Little said, "I saw it and I read it and I've been afraid this would happen all along. And now we're going straight to the authorities."

"Wait for me," honked Lucille Goose, and flapping her big wings madly, she ran down the lane after them.

They came to a path in the woods, and there they met Waily Quaily, who was always crying about something. "Why are you all coming after me?" asked Waily Quaily defensively.

"We're not coming after you," honked Lucille Goose. "A bill is passing that will compel us to hire foxes in the henhouse, and we're going to complain to the king."

"That's not half as bad as the movie I'm protesting," whined Waily Quaily. "It's really terrible."

"Have you seen it yet?" asked Chicken Little.

"No, but I just know it's terrible and will be the end of the barnyard as we know it. I'll go with you and we can protest together."

So the whole group headed toward the castle of the king—but soon they came upon Foxy Woxy.

"Where are all you fine folks going in such a hurry?" asked Foxy Woxy.

"A bill is passing and a bad movie is being made," said Chicken Little. "We are going to let our voices be heard."

"Why don't you just start a letter-writing campaign?" said Foxy Woxy. "You could send faxes and telegrams and jam the king's switchboard with calls of outrage."

"Oh dear," clucked Chicken Little. "Why didn't we think of that earlier?"

"If you'll come over to my cave," Foxy Woxy said invitingly, "I'll give you access to my media center and you can set up your headquarters there."

Everyone agreed to the blitz. Foxy Woxy went ahead, and the others followed in line. They were almost to his home when they met Wordy Birdy.

"What a lovely day for a walk," she called. "May I ask where you are going?"

"Oh dear, a bill is passing," said Chicken Little, "and a terrible movie is being made. We're all going to speak our mind to the king and let him know how powerful we are against these terrible developments."

"And how do you know a bill is passing?" asked Wordy Birdy.

"Because I saw it and I read it and I've been afraid this would happen all along."

"May I see a copy of the legislation?" asked Wordy Birdy.

Chicken Little handed her a photocopy, and Wordy Birdy clicked her tongue against her beak. "Oh dear," she said.

"What's the matter?" said Cocky Locky. "Don't you think we have enough clout to stop it? I have a friend in the cabinet, you know."

"My chicks are in danger!" said Henny Penny.

"My geese are cooked if this goes through," said Lucille Goose.

"Everyone's against me," whined Waily Quaily.

"We've got to get to the phones and faxes now," barked Foxy Woxy.

In her wise way, Wordy Birdy motioned with her wing for them to stop. "This is simply a photocopy of the same bill that's been distributed for years and years," said she. "It's not real."

"And what about the movie?" whined Waily Quaily.

"Again, it's a rumor that's run around here for quite some time."

"Then we got all worked up for nothing?" asked Chicken Little.

"I'm afraid so," said Wordy Birdy. "Your heavenly Father knows your frame and understands. Who of you by worrying can add a single hour to your life? As a matter of fact, you will surely be eaten if you continue on this path."

So Chicken Little, Henny Penny, Cocky Locky, Groggy Froggy, Waily Quaily and Lucille Goose ran back to the barnyard.

As Wordy Birdy flew away, she noticed Foxy Woxy shaking his paw at her and lamenting her advice. For it was Foxy Woxy who had planted the bill in the barnyard and spread the movie rumor to strike fear into the animals and make them his noontime feast.

COMPULSIVELLA

nce upon a time there lived a man whose wife died. Jumping into another relationship much too quickly, he married a woman who was mean—and her two daughters were worse. So he spent most of his time at work or sitting in on board meetings at church and being an absentee father.

This caused deep scars for his own kind and lovely daughter Ella. It also meant she bore the brunt of dysfunction in this blended family.

No sooner had the mother and daughters moved in than the stepmother began tearing down what little self-esteem Ella possessed. But the woman did commend Ella's habit of cleaning everything, and this cast the poor girl into an obsession.

Ella washed the dishes, scrubbed the stairs, polished the floors, cleaned the stove and did it all without realizing she was looking for approval. Every night she took her fifteen-minute-meal-for-busy-women container from the freezer for herself, then cooked a balanced dinner for the family.

After washing and drying the dishes, she cleaned cinders from the chimney for further validation. Because of this her stepsisters thought of nicknaming her "Cinderella," but Ella thought this was too beautiful a name for the likes of her. The sisters decided that "Compulsivella" was a better fit.

It happened that the most eligible bachelor in town, the parson's son, invited all the young ladies of the kingdom to a nondenominational church picnic. Whoever baked the tastiest item for dinner would be his bride. The sisters planned their menus and outfits carefully. As a codependent, Compulsivella volunteered her time so she could keep everyone happy.

"Aren't you going to the picnic?" asked the sisters. "You're dressed perfectly for the sack race."

"The parson's son would never marry me," Compulsivella moaned. "I'm so ugly, and besides it's been three weeks since I dusted behind the refrigerator. There's just so much to do."

The long-awaited evening came at last, and the two proud sisters stepped into a beautiful carriage and rode away to the picnic. Alone with her mop, Compulsivella was caught in a mire of negative thinking. To lift her spirits she turned on the radio.

The dial was set to a counseling program, and the host seemed to be talking directly to her. She called his 800 number and was on the air in a matter of minutes.

"Thank you for your call," the man said after listening to her story. "Are you seeing a counselor?"

"I don't deserve one," Compulsivella said. "I can't afford in-patient care, and when I call in to programs like this I wind up cleaning the earpiece on the phone."

"Do not despair," he said gently. "I'll be your fairy therapist. I can help solve all your problems. Now tell me about your childhood."

The fairy therapist soon knew Compulsivella's whole story. Because she used her real name and not "Anonymous," so did the rest of the kingdom.

"I only know what you've told me," said the fairy therapist. "And this advice should not be substituted for professional help, but I think you want to go to the picnic."

"How did you know that?" Compulsivella gasped.

"Trust me," he said. "Go to the garden and get a pumpkin."

Compulsivella wondered how this could possibly help, but she hurried to the garden, brought back the largest organically grown pumpkin, cleaned it off thoroughly and set it on the table.

"This pumpkin represents all your hurtful relationships and the shame of your past," the radio therapist said. "I want you to strike it now and get out your aggression. Feel free to scream through your rage."

Compulsivella did as her fairy therapist said, and soon the pumpkin was pulverized. "That felt pretty good," Compulsivella said. "What do I do now?"

"Bake a pie with what is left and take it to the picnic," the fairy therapist said. "You're a winner! You can do it! And you're very important to me. Now let me put you on hold, we have a commercial break coming."

Compulsivella did not waste any time baking the pie, and what a pie it was. But when the therapist's voice returned, she gave vent to her anxiety: "What will I wear? I have only rags."

"When was the last time you bought something nice for yourself?" the fairy therapist asked.

"I can't remember when," she said.

"Exactly! You wear rags because you think you're not a valuable person. Go out immediately and spend some money on a nice outfit. Tell yourself you are a good person. Get out of the downward cycle and get the spiral going upward.

"But be careful," he warned. "When you hear the clock strike midnight, you must leave because your love tank will need refilling. And don't forget to pay off your credit card quickly, or you'll experience a massive amount of consumer debt."

"How do you know that?" asked Compulsivella.

"I'm also a fairy financial counselor."

"I will pay it off," Compulsivella promised. But when she maxed out her VISA with an expensive dress and shoes, she actually launched the first bout in what would become a long fight with shopaholism.

As she walked toward the picnic grounds, a murmur of admiration fluttered through the crowd. "How striking she is," everyone said.

The parson's son took the pie from her and set her at the place of honor. Since dancing was not allowed, they played a fast game of Uno until the feast was prepared. Because the young man was visually oriented, he hardly touched his meal—so taken was he with Compulsivella's beauty.

When dessert came and the pumpkin pie was served, the clock struck eleven. Compulsivella's breathing became irregular, and she realized she was having a panic attack. She stood up, curtsied and ran away. (She would later discover, during a group session, that her self-esteem was still dangerously low and she was repressing a memory about a faulty alarm clock.)

Soon after she returned home, her stepmother and stepsisters entered. "If you had been to the picnic, you would have seen the most beautiful princess ever," said one sister.

"No one knows her name, but the parson's son is very interested in her," said the other.

Compulsivella was so overjoyed that she put down her security vacuum. The next day the parson's son came riding through the village with the half-eaten pumpkin pie, a pathetic sight indeed.

"If anyone can identify this pie and prove she made it," he shouted through a flood of tears, "I will straightaway marry her, and we shall live happily ever after."

Though Compulsivella heard the call, she was too wounded and needy to respond. The stepsisters heaped false guilt upon her and asked her to help them make a pie to fool the parson's son. As usual she complied, giving them way too much control. But this second pie was not the same, because Compulsivella had not embraced the pain that led to the creation of the first glorious pie.

The parson's son returned home without the mystery woman. Compulsivella became absorbed with herself, but after a while she went back to her group meetings.

One week she noticed a handsome but poorly dressed young man cowering in the corner of the church basement where the group met. To her surprise it was the parson's son. He was dealing with PDD, Princess Deficit Disorder.

A few months later, the parson performed the wedding ceremony live on the fairy therapist's daily program. Compulsivella and her new husband started a small group ministry and made plans to release their first teaching video.

Since they learned to lower their expectations for each other, they have lived happily ever after, though Compulsivella continues to deal with her credit history and the adverse effects of living with a "messy."

THE LITTLE
RED HEN

iligence and faithfulness were the hallmarks of the Little Red Hen. She lived in a church-sponsored apartment complex that brought together animals from differing ethnic and socio-economic strata.

The pig, the duck and the cat dwelled with her, but alas, they never did anything for the church. The pig liked to wallow in the mud and recite verses, the duck enjoyed the pond and quacked a few bars of favorite hymns, and the cat purred on the patio in the sunshine.

One day the Little Red Hen found a decision card lying on the ground.

"Who will help me follow up this needy soul?" she asked.

"Not I," grunted the pig from the mud. "I'm working on my memory verse for the week, Proverbs 11:22."

"Not I," quacked the duck from the pond. "I'm only on the third stanza of 'Make Me a Blessing.'" And she sang, "Give as 'twas given to you in your need . . ."

"Not I," purred the cat. "But I'll certainly pray for you."

So the Little Red Hen set off and made contact with the mare who had filled out the decision card. The horse was truly repentant, and so the Little Red Hen began discipling her.

The next week the Little Red Hen was cleaning the house when the pastor called and asked her to teach a Sunday-school class.

"My, but I'm awfully busy," said the Little Red Hen. "But the tiny ones need a teacher desperately. If I can't find someone else, I'll do it."

"Who will help teach Sunday school?" asked the Little Red Hen.

"Not I," yawned the pig. "It's not my spiritual gift."

"Not I," quacked the duck. "I don't like the songs they sing."

"Not I," purred the cat. "I'm prioritizing my life."

"Very well then, I will teach them myself," said the Little Red Hen. Carefully she prepared each week's lesson, collected yarn for craft time, discipled the mare and kept up with her daily chores.

Soon the Little Red Hen was running to and fro like a chicken with its . . . like the very busy chicken she was, when the doorbell rang. It was Mrs. Goose from across the courtyard, who was in charge of the piglet nursery.

"I don't see how I can possibly do another thing," sighed the Little Red Hen.

"But if you don't, we'll have to endure the grunting of so many little piglets in the worship service."

"We can't have that," said the Little Red Hen. "If I can't find someone to help, I'll do it."

By now the Little Red Hen was all but losing her sanctification toward the others, and the tone of her voice nearly scared one of the cat's lives completely out of her.

"Who will help in the nursery this week?" yelled the Little Red Hen.

"Not I," said the pig. "I am doing the Scripture reading."

"Not I," intoned the duck. "I have special music during the offertory."

"Not I," mewed the cat. "I am allergic to the filthy things."

"Very well," said the Little Red Hen. "I will do it myself."

Sunday afternoon came, and the Little Red Hen was lying in a heap on the kitchen floor, suffering from severe burnout. She was so exhausted she could not rise to make dinner for the household.

She heard a knock at the door and raised her head just in time to see the mare, her pastor and Mrs. Goose bringing a plate of fresh bread, hot corn on the cob and an apple pie.

"This is for your hard work and diligence," the three said. "You have been such an encouragement to us that we wanted to encourage you." And with that they left as quickly as they had come.

The cat, the duck and the pig appeared at the window, sniffing at the air hungrily.

"Who will help me eat my dinner?" asked the Little Red Hen.

"I will," grunted the pig.

"I will," quacked the duck.

"I'd rather have tuna, but I guess I will," purred the cat.

"I followed up the decision card," said the Little Red Hen. "I taught Sunday school, and I helped out with the piglets in nursery. You three recited verses, sang and lay in the sun while I kept busy."

"Aw, come on, Little Red Hen," the pig said. "You know we're not as mature as you. Have a heart. We've learned our lesson." The duck and cat agreed.

"If I didn't care for you I would gladly offer you an equal portion of my bounty," the Little Red Hen said. "However, I do care and wish you to change your behavior."

And the Little Red Hen practiced tough love that day and ate the bread, the corn and the pie all by herself.

BEAUTY & THE
MARK OF THE BEAST

nce upon a time there was a sweet-dispositioned young girl named Beauty who followed all the passing fads in her Christian world. At this point in her life she was very much into angels. She had figurines by her bedside, pictures of angels on her walls and bookshelves filled with angel tomes from every publisher under the sun.

Her father was a wealthy, respected merchant and a member in good standing with the Believer's Business Men's Committee. He read all the current books about excellence and believed success followed the committed Christian wherever he went.

Alas, when Beauty began buying golden angel earrings and necklaces with ruby seraphs, his fortune was soon lost, and he could not bring himself to go to the meetings.

One day word arrived that a sailing vessel filled with his multilevel sales products had come to port, and he was filled with great hopes of returning to his upper-middle-class lifestyle.

"What would you like me to bring back to you, Beauty?" her father asked.

"Only yourself, Father," she replied. "And maybe a book about the end times. I think prophecy is going to heat up again, so I'd better read up on it."

When he reached the port and located his ship, he set up meetings and asked everyone to list three things they've always dreamed of owning. However, he could sell none of the merchandise and failed to recruit any local distributors, so he junked the ship and declared bankruptcy. For him it truly was an economic earthquake. Realizing he would never be asked to speak at a success seminar, he dejectedly made his way home.

In the deep forest he lost his way in a furious thunderstorm. In a flash of lightning, he was relieved to spy a mansion on a nearby hilltop. When no one answered his knock at the door, he pushed it open, calling, "Hello? I'm a financially challenged entrepreneur on his way home, and I'm in need of shelter."

Not a soul came, so he helped himself to dinner. When he finished he went upstairs to thank the generous host. He found not a living soul, but in a guest room he discovered a budgeting guide and a newsletter detailing the latest investment strategies. On the other side of the room he was amazed to see an entire wall of shelves filled with hundreds of books about eschatology. There were numerous books on the Second Coming and the tribulation period, along with posters of the rapture.

He found a book with an angel pictured on the front and picked it from the shelf. When he turned to leave, he heard a terrifying shriek, and a hideous figure stood before him. The man wore a polyester suit, and a pocket protector protruded from his shirt. He was balding but had combed his thin hair forward from the back.

"You ungrateful guest! How dare you!" the man roared. "After I give you food and shelter and some budgeting tips, you steal from my most prized possession? I just knew it would come to this. The signs are everywhere."

"I did not know," said the father. "I am a poor merchant and was only taking this home for my beautiful daughter, who expressed interest in eschatological things."

"Is she a New Ager?" asked the man.

"Of course not; she's a very devout young lady."

"Is she a member of the Trilateral Commission?"

"Certainly not," the father answered. "Her hobby is angels, and she buys many trinkets."

"Well, if you're so destitute, how does she purchase them?" asked the man.

"I am sorry to say she charges them."

Again the man shrieked and covered his face. "Don't you know the credit card is the precursor to the mark? First came MasterCard, then the bar codes. Tomorrow they come for me."

"I promise to cut them in half as soon as I return home, but please let me take this book to my daughter."

"If she really wants to read it, let her come here," said the owner. "But if you do not bring her back, I'll know you're part of the Illuminati."

Beauty's father returned home and explained the problem. She consented to go with him to the castle, spend some days in fellowship with its owner and prove she knew nothing of these conspiracies.

When they walked in, Beauty was listening to a contemporary song about angels on her headset. The man shrieked, "Subliminal messages!"

Those first few days were quite tenuous for Beauty and the homeowner, but they made it through. Beauty read more and more about prophecy and made plans to attend several conferences. Gradually her love grew for the man in polyester, but there were still many communication problems. When they argued the man shrieked like a wild animal, and that is why Beauty called him "the Beast."

"Beast," she said one day affectionately, "I've been down to the bookstore and have purchased several titles about relationships. Don't you think we need to improve our communication?"

"What do you mean?" said the Beast.

"Well, you're a microwave and I'm a crock pot. You think visually and I think with my emotions."

"I don't think we have a problem," said the Beast.

"Denial ain't just a river in Egypt," she said.

So they stopped discussing the ashes of the red heifer and focused on word pictures. "Let me understand what you're saying," the Beast learned to say. And then he would state his version of what she had said.

As they grew to accept each other's flaws, Beauty discovered she was falling in love with the Beast. They went through many hours of premarital counseling and a couples' retreat before they wed.

As a shared hobby they took up the study of temperaments and discovered Beauty was a "phlegmatic/cocker spaniel" and the Beast was a "melan-collie."

As they had more and more children, Beauty and the Beast began to focus on their family. They went through many books on the strong-willed child and found out that parenting isn't for cowards. They learned not to make idle threats about punishment and instituted a time-out rule.

The Beast, a firstborn, sang choruses at men's retreats while Beauty immersed herself in Christian romance novels. Their love was strong and took them through many other prevailing trends in the subculture.

However, Beauty never did get over her fascination with angels and credit cards. And the Beast, though he worked on his tone of voice, remained quite loud. It's sad to say, but after the birth of each child he crept into the nursery and checked under the bonnet of his new baby for any sign of a beastly mark.

In spite of all their foibles and fads, the two lived relatively happily ever after.

RUMPELBOOKSELLER

very poor but sincere Christian speaker/author traveled with his daughter, who sang, played the piano and had a badly produced CD. Because of his desire to reach more people with his message, he went to speak with a publisher. Losing his head in the process, he told the editorial committee that his daughter had the ability to spin gold out of overstocked books.

"That's quite a spiritual gift," the editors said. "If your daughter is that clever, bring her to the warehouse tomorrow so we may put her to the test."

This vexed the daughter mightily, because she wasn't even able to sell her own CDs, let alone unsold books. But after throwing a tantrum, she consented to help her distressed father.

When the girl arrived the next day, they led her into a room full of biographies by professional athletes and recording artists.

"Now set to work," they requested, "and if by early morning you have not changed these books into money, we won't give your father a contract."

So the poor pastor's daughter was left alone. She had no idea what to do, and her heart ached so much that she began to weep.

Suddenly she heard a noise at the window. When she opened it, in leaped a small man who was—well, to be kind, not a looker. He was not gifted with height, and he grinned from ear to ear.

"What's the matter with you?" he said.

"I am a poor piano player who can't even sell my own music, and my father has promised I can sell these books by morning. It's hopeless."

"I can do it," said the man.

"What's it going to cost me?"

"Your piano will do," he answered.

As soon as the girl agreed, he picked up the phone and made a quick demographic survey, fired off a few direct fax appeals and spun his sales with lightning speed. The girl fell asleep in the corner, and when she woke up the man was gone. To her amazement, so were all the books.

At sunrise the editors came and rejoiced at the girl's work, for they were very conscious of their inventory. They took her to a warehouse that was twice the size of the first room and said, "If you can move these, we'll even publish your father's novel."

When the door had been shut and locked, the girl saw that the room was filled with biographies of older sports stars with bad knees who had become singers. It was a very difficult lot.

The girl slumped into despair once more—but soon she heard a familiar sound at the window. In popped the little man, with the same grin on his face. "Before you begin," she said, "I have nothing left to pay you. The piano was my treasure, but it is yours."

"Then you must promise me the first royalty check and the advance from the sale of your father's first parenting book."

That sounded quite reasonable to the girl, but then the man added, "Plus you must promise me your firstborn child."

Well, who knows whether I will ever have a child at all? thought the girl. Since she had no alternative and figured she could bring a lawsuit if necessary, she promised the man what he desired.

Immediately he began spinning the books to potential buyers. He booked three cruises filled with fans of aged singing sports stars and a boat full of gerontologists. By the next morning all the books were gone.

When the editors arrived, they were quite happy and offered her father a contract on the spot.

Not long after that the girl married, and a year later she had a wonderful child. The infant had a high Apgar score and was teething with molars by its first birthday. By this time the girl's father's fame had grown, for his teaching truly was sound. He had his own radio program, a newsletter and three bestsellers, and his first book on parenting was due in the fall. Having learned from his previous mistakes, he passed along great parenting wisdom to his daughter.

Just before the child's birthday party began, the girl heard a sound at her window. When she opened it, she found the smiling little man.

"What do you want?" she asked.

"I have come for my due," he said. "You promised the advance and first royalty check from your father's book."

The daughter was terrified, because she knew he would ask for the child next. "How about giving me three days and letting me guess your name?"

"Are you kidding?" said the man. "A deal's a deal. Hand over the money, and don't forget to include the baby."

With the child wailing in the background, the girl began to smile. The wisdom imparted by her father was about to pay off. "OK," she said, "but if you take the money and the child, you have to keep them. Return one and you lose rights to the other."

The little man agreed, and the girl made him sign his name—which proved to be Rumpelbookseller—

on a hastily drawn contract of her own. He took the royalty check and the child and disappeared through the window.

However, diaper changing, midnight feedings, teething pain, constant crying, formula mixing and added laundry soon brought the little man to the realization that being a full-time mom is a lot like spinning straw into gold. It's hard work, and you get no recognition from society.

He returned the next day with bloodshot eyes. "I can't take it anymore," he said, and handed over the child and the check. It was the first time the girl had seen Rumpelbookseller without a smile on his face. And she has never heard from him since.

HANSEL & GRETEL

ear a great forest there lived a poor cutter of wood whose company was down-sizing because of a family of spotted owls. He and his wife were in the sandwich years and worried not only about their two children but also about their aging parents. The children, Hansel and Gretel, were both home-schooled.

Since school vouchers were not available, the parents had no control over their educational dollars. They were heavily taxed by the current administration and could afford only a small house in a shabby neighborhood. They had a compact car, rarely went out to eat and had to settle for basic cable, no premium channels.

One fitful night the father lay in bed thinking, turning and tossing. His resolve for home-schooling was waning under the intense financial pressure. Finally he said to his wife, "What will become of us? If you don't go out into the workplace and bring in another income, we won't be able to afford a bigger house."

"Maybe you can get a second job," she replied. "Can't you become more than a carpenter?"

"I am stretched to the limit," he said. "I think I have repetitive stress syndrome as it is."

"We can't afford to send the children to a Christian school," answered the wife. "If I am to go out, we will have to send them to public school, and we will need a second car."

"It will be a great sacrifice," the husband said, "but I will take public transportation and you can have the car."

"Agreed," said the wife. "Early in the morning we will provide Hansel and Gretel with their lunch. We will take them to the schoolyard and leave them until late in the afternoon."

"But wife," said the man, "if we leave them in such an environment, the secular humanists may devour their little minds. Outcome-based education could scar them forever. It may be increasingly difficult to pass along our values, and perhaps the two will grow up unable to distinguish right from wrong."

"But," she countered, "if we keep home-schooling and I do not find a job, we'll stay in this dingy home with its one-car garage the rest of our lives."

"Good point," he said. "I'm probably overreacting. Besides, there's always quality time."

The walls were so thin in the house that Hansel and Gretel had heard every word. Gretel began to cry.

"Don't worry, Gretel," Hansel said. "I have a plan."

The next morning the mother said, "Rise and shine, children; we have a special field trip planned. It's social interaction day, and you're going to meet many new friends." When Hansel and Gretel did not get up, their mother counted to three several times. Finally they dragged themselves out of bed and got dressed.

As the family walked along toward school, Hansel tore pieces from his low-cholesterol peanut-butter-and-jelly sandwich and dropped them on the ground.

When they reached the playground, the father and mother patted their heads and bid them goodby.

"Rest yourselves here, children," he said. "Mother and I will come back for you soon. If we're not back by three-thirty, take the bus."

So Hansel and Gretel sat by the swingset and had an early lunch while they watched the other children play. When the bell called the schoolchildren inside, the two followed the sandwich trail home.

There they whiled away the hours singing along with their audiotape collection until their parents returned.

The next day the parents returned them to the school with money for a hot lunch. This time Hansel pulled offering envelopes from his pocket and dropped them at intervals along the road. (Hansel scribbled on these each Sunday morning and had quite a collection.)

But Hansel ran out of envelopes while they were still a good way from the school, and when they were ready to go home they were unable to find the trail. So they wandered the school hallways until they saw a cheery classroom decorated with colorful drawings. A middle-aged woman came to the door and beckoned them inside.

"Come," she said, "we are beginning the first chapter in our new reader, *Heather Has Lots of Cousins, Too.*"

Gretel sat at the back of the class and watched the children misspell words while Hansel went to the reading circle. "This is whole language, deary," the teacher whispered to her. Then she wrote on Gretel's slate, "I no ure gong to luv it."

Later, when the bus dropped Hansel and Gretel at home, the father and mother greeted their children and debriefed them.

"What was the best part of your day, Gretel?" asked her mother.

"I liked the spelling bee," she said.

"Did you win?" the father said, for he was very grade-conscious.

"Of course not," said Gretel. "There are no winners or losers. We all received ribbons for participation, because competition damages the psyches of those who are alphabetically challenged."

"I see," said her mother. "What did you learn today, Hansel?"

"In science I learned I am only a little more advanced than animals. We have all been taught our parents' myths about religion and life. But best of all, I came to understand why you and Father sent us to the wonderful new school."

"And why is that?" asked his father.

"We played a game called Lifeboat," he said. "And now I understand that Gretel and I are simply learning to swim."

So Hansel and Gretel tried their best to adapt to their new surroundings. The family did move up to a four-bedroom bungalow with a two-car garage and pool in the back. They upgraded their cable subscription and ate dinner out more often. But the parents were so busy they had little time to ponder the effects of their commitment to income-based education.

THE FISHERMAN
& HIS CONGREGATION

faithful pastor who tried hard to keep his work and family life balanced loved to fish on his day off. The stroll to the lake and the fresh air made him forget the weight and worry of his small congregation. Though he loved to fish, he rarely caught anything.

One beautiful Monday morning he baited his hook and cast it far into the lake. Immediately he felt a strong tug and reeled in an enormous fish. But before he could take the hook out, the fish looked at him and said, "Pray let me live, good sir. I am really an enchanted man formerly known as a prince; I only appear to be a Northern Pike. Put me back in the water and let me go."

"I could never hurt a talking fish," the pastor said. "Swim away in peace." So the fish left him.

At the board meeting the next day the pastor said, "What a grand fish I caught yesterday. He said he was an enchanted prince."

"What did you do with him?" asked the head of the board.

"I threw him back," replied the pastor.

"You didn't ask him for anything?"

"No. What should I have asked for?"

"Ah," groaned the deacon. "We worship in this hovel of a church with leaky pipes and a hissing radiator. Our nursery is musty, we have no kitchen to speak of, and our songbooks are falling apart. Go back and tell the fish we want a beautiful sanctuary and some new hymnals."

The pastor did not like the idea, but he was terrified of the leadership of the church. So he stood at the water's edge and called,

"O fish that I caught,
I'm in water that's hot.
There's none in the nation
Like my congregation
That sends me to beg of thee."

The fish came swimming to him and asked, "What does your congregation want?"

"They say I should have asked you for a new sanctuary and, if you could spare them, some nice new hymnals to replace the old ones."

"Go back to the church then," said the fish. "They are in the sanctuary already."

When he returned he saw huge stained-glass windows, a fountain flowing from the baptistery and sparkling red hymnals in the racks on the back of each cushioned pew.

Everyone was quite pleased for about a week. After the service the next Sunday, the pastor was greeting people when a member whispered in his ear, "The sermons you give are not seeker-friendly."

"And what would you have me to do?" asked the pastor.

"Go back to the fish and ask him for a new computer and a CD/ROM version of *Complete Pastoral Stories and Illustrations for the Unchurched*," said the member.

Though he hated asking the fish for another favor, the pastor went back and called out toward the water,

"O fish that I caught,

I'm in water that's hot.

There are constant frustrations

With my illustrations,

So they've sent me again to thee."

"What is it this time?" asked the fish.

"I need to be more seeker-friendly so that we might bring more unchurched into the services," said the pastor. "Could you possibly spare a few multimedia aids that might bring my technique up to speed?"

"Very well," said the fish. "Your new computer is already there, and the software is preloaded."

The following Sunday the pastor's message was "Fifteen Minutes to an Eternal Relationship." The sermon was well received because it was filled with stories, illustrations and pop culture allusions, and, of course, it lasted only fifteen minutes.

All went well until Wednesday night, when several urgent personal needs were brought to the pastor's attention.

"We need you to counsel these individuals and help them overcome their problems," one elder said.

"How can I spend time with my seeker-friendly message, get the church's administrative work done, be a good husband and father, and still counsel all these by myself?" the poor pastor asked.

"We'll send you to a men's conference next year with thousands of others who are in their warrior stage," said the elder. "For right now go tell the fish to make you a good counselor."

The fish was waiting at the edge of the water with his fin on his chin. "Back so soon?" he said.

"Yes, my church wants my total commitment to counsel our members," the pastor said. "My days are filled with message preparation, administrative chores and visitation, and they still want me to be God's man in the family with perfect children and a Proverbs 31 wife."

"Have you been to any men's conferences?" said the fish.

"I'm supposed to go next year," answered the pastor.

"Until then, I've provided you with Micro-Psych, the new Windows counseling software, and your wife can now accompany you on the piano."

The pastor returned home and found these improvements. He also discovered that both his children suddenly had beautiful smiles and could recite numerous memory verses through their pearly white teeth.

Alas, the congregation still was not happy.

"We want to be the number-one church," said a member who was very into church growth statistics. "My research shows we can achieve a 300 percent growth spurt with a new gymnasium, professional musicians, lasers, a five-state bus ministry and a drive-in theater that broadcasts our service from a huge parking lot."

"Don't you think that's a bit much?" asked the pastor. "We're having a hard time keeping track of all the people as it is. Plus, how could we take an offering with all those people at the drive-in?"

"Haven't you ever heard of in-line skates?" asked the member. "It's a perfect ministry for our teens."

Though he tried, the pastor could not talk the church out of sending him to the fish again.

"O fish in the lake,
You may think me a flake
To ask for a union
With a skating communion,

But they say we'll be number one."

"Let me guess," said the fish. "Church growth?"

"How did you know?" said the pastor.

"I saw some of your members fishing yesterday in a stream north of here that's lined with willows. It's a very nice creek, but it's a mistake to make it run through your particular church setting."

"I wish I could convince them otherwise," said the pastor.

So the fish gave them all they asked, and the church became number one in the entire kingdom. Articles were published about it in major news magazines. But with all their success, the people of the congregation couldn't sleep for thinking what they could do next.

A group of concerned members gathered one morning for breakfast and decided to ask for a king to be appointed from the church who would have absolute rule.

"Can't we be content with being number one?" said the pastor. "We had twenty-five thousand people last weekend!" But the members would not relent.

As he approached the lake, black clouds gathered and thunder roared overhead. Lightning flashed, and the fish appeared on the water. The pastor trembled before him.

"They want a king," said the pastor.

"A king?" said the fish. "Go back to them and rejoice, because they have needed this all along."

When the pastor returned, he was astonished. The stained glass was gone. The buses, the parking lot, the theater screen, the gymnasium and most of the people were gone too. In their place, restored to its original condition, was their little church.

Today the congregation worships there in humility. Every time they sing from their battered hymnals or hear the leaky radiator clang, they thank the true King for their pastor and promise not to ask so much of him ever again.

THE EMPEROR'S
NEW BIBLE

any years ago there lived an Emperor who cared much for the outer things of man. He loved good food, fine clothes and a steady coach that got many miles per slave. He also loved to accumulate Bibles, though he did not spend much time reading them. He kept them hidden in his innermost chamber and admired them each night before going to bed.

One day two unsavory characters arrived in his great city and proclaimed themselves translators of Holy Writ. Hearing of their expertise, the Emperor had them brought to his royal chambers.

"I have many translations, amplifications, paraphrases and commentaries," the Emperor said. "I have a One-Year Bible, a One-Week Bible, a One-Minute Bible for People on the Go and a Thirty-Second Bible for People on the Go with Incredibly Small Attention Spans. Can you possibly give me anything new?"

"We can, Your Majesty," the wily thieves said. "We have been reimagining a translation that will delight all those who are rightcous and inclusive in their language. Those who understand intellectual things will find this work unique in all the world. Those who do not are simply not very spiritual. Alas, all we need are the funds to get a committee together."

So the Emperor gave the two rascals a wad of cash, and they began work at once. The two demanded the richest ink and the oldest manuscripts. Valuable heirlooms were brought to them at a moment's notice and were never seen again.

I should like to know how far they have gotten, thought the Emperor one day. But he was afraid that among the committee's elite minds he might not understand the translation and thus would prove himself to be unspiritual. *I will send my honest Minister of Theology to the translators,* he thought.

The Minister of Theology, a long-nosed gentleman with great bushy eyebrows, walked into the hall. The two men were scribbling the following words on the royal blackboard:

Philippians 4:13: I can do all things through my own efforts, because the Lord helps those who help themselves.

"Mercy preserve us!" said the Minister of Theology. "You've changed the entire verse."

"We don't want religion to be a crutch," said the men. "People should stop believing fables and take responsibility for their lives."

The Minister went closer and found that all masculine references to God were changed from "He" to "He/She" and, where appropriate, to "The Eternal It."

Can I indeed be unspiritual? thought the Minister. *Not a soul must know I cannot see the sense of this translation.* So the Minister of Theology left the men and gave a fine report to the Emperor.

The thieves asked for more money to help in their work. This time the Emperor sent it along with an honest statesman who was a member of the Emperor's yearly prayer breakfast.

"Look at our latest translations," the men said when the statesman entered the hall.

On the blackboard he saw the following verse:

Romans 3:23: For all have made negative choices in their lives and are not living up to their own expectations.

"We have changed the Romans Road to the Romans Path to Peace and Prosperity," said the men. And they pointed to the next verse, which read thus:

Romans 6:23: The payment for negative choices in life is low self-esteem, but the gift of The Eternal It is self-fulfillment in all you do. You deserve a break.

The statesman was aghast at what he saw, yet he did not want anyone thinking him unspiritual or opposed to scholarly pursuits. He too gave a good report to the Emperor.

All the people of the town were talking about the new Bible. Animal rights activists were overjoyed that Old Testament sacrifices were being changed to tree-planting ceremonies. Feminists who had long complained to the Emperor about the authoritarian nature of the Scriptures were delighted in the translation of 1 Timothy 2:12: "I do not permit a woman to teach or to have authority over a man, unless she really feels like it."

All references to sin were plucked out. All references to hell were supplanted with positive statements of God's love. The new Scriptures did not banish the unregenerate to outer darkness but affirmed "everyone who is really sincere in their belief system."

The miracles of Jesus were gone. References to Lazarus' rising from the dead and to Jesus' resurrection were deleted so as not to offend those who were resurrection-impaired.

At last the scoundrels bound their slim-line work with an attractive leather cover and presented it to the Emperor. He was so thrilled with the job they had done that he said, "I'll give you something extra if you'll prepare an Emperor's Study Edition. I would also love for you to take a look at our hymnal. It seems so outdated by comparison." The two accepted gladly.

The Emperor's counselors suggested that he sponsor a public reading of the text for the entire kingdom. "What a splendid idea," he said, and a great procession was held in honor of the completed work.

The royal orator produced the meager text with a flourish and began to read from Genesis. "In the beginning," he read, "and over billions of years and much evolution, The Eternal It created heaven and earth." The footnotes pointed out that the Bible is not a textbook and the original creation account was simply metaphorical.

Particularly well received were the stories of Noah and the local flood, Moses and the Ten Suggestions, and the survival of the three Hebrew children who were thrown into a hot tub at Nebuchadnezzar's spa.

When the orator made it to the New Testament, Jesus had very little to say. The flawed account of Judas was changed because he was, after all, simply a financial opportunist working within his own moral frame of reference.

The crowd cheered the reading. The Emperor applauded. But on the edge of the square sat a small child who listened intently to the words. Finally he could take it no longer and cried out above the din,

"The Emperor has no Bible! These are not the words I have been taught."

A murmur went through the crowd. One whispered to another what the child had said. "The lad is right," said a father. "These are not the words of our Lord."

The Emperor, who had been heeding the excellent delivery of the orator and not the content, approached the lad. "You are questioning the work done on the texts?" he said.

"Your Majesty," answered the boy, "if you will but read from my Bible and compare the words, you will understand."

The boy pulled a shabby old book from his pocket and handed it to the Emperor. "For the wages of sin is death," the Emperor read, "but the gift of God is eternal life in Christ Jesus our Lord."

Upon reading the text the ruler suddenly felt naked before the crowd. It was the first time he had read these words as anything but literature. He grabbed the new translation and tore it in half, then commanded that the scoundrels be thrown from the kingdom.

Through the faithful witness of one small boy, the Emperor was saved from spiritual ruin. And from that day forward the Emperor did not merely collect God's Word but began reading it, living it and hiding it in his heart, which he found to be much better than keeping it on his bedroom shelf.

THE PIED PIPER
OF FIRST CHURCH

here is a tiny village near you named Hamelin, and most of the residents attend First Church and many sing in the choir. The Melody River runs by the town's southern wall and continues through less quaint towns.

Not too long ago the people of Hamelin were having an awful time. The problem was music! The choir sang great hymns of the faith with much breath support and stunning arrangements. But the baby boomers wanted more contemporary tunes with guitars and synthesizers. The children were too young to understand and were content to sing "Jesus Loves Me."

The clamor between the two factions became so great that a delegation from each group met the church staff in the pastor's study.

"Why can't we hear our kind of music in the service?" cried the boomers. "We want relevance. We want something with a little life and a beat so we can invite our friends."

"Why should we get rid of our great heritage for some praise choruses?" said the choir director. "Your friends don't need sugarcoated lyrics, they need substance."

On and on the argument went, until there was a knock at the door. A cheerful voice drawled, "May I come in?"

"Enter," said the exasperated pastor. The man who entered looked quite odd. He was tall and fit, for he used the latest Christian exercise videos regularly. Under his arm he carried an electric guitar, and behind him he pulled a roadcase containing synthesizers and effects boxes.

"Sir," he said to the pastor, "I have an answer to your musical problem. I'm often called on to rid a community of vermin, snakes, ants and people of the older demographic. But in this case I believe I can soothe both factions in your church and teach them eternal things as well."

"What is your name?" the pastor asked.

"I used to be known as the Pied Piper," the man said. "Of course my pipe is digitally sampled now, but you can't go around as the Pied Keyboardist or the Pied Lead Guitarist, so I'm sticking with Piper."

"What will it cost us?" asked a staff member on the finance board.

"This gig will be difficult, but we can talk about royalties and residuals later," the Piper replied. "First let me show you what I can do."

The group watched in amazement as the Piper plugged his guitar into an amplifier, opened his road-case and began wailing strains of a contemporary "Amazing Grace."

Footsteps pounded through the church hallway, and an army of youngsters crowded around the study. Baby boomers shoved and leaped over one another to get close to the sound. The steeple rocked and the church bells chimed as the drum machine banged out its rhythm.

The young crowd was overjoyed to hear music that spoke to their souls. But the old guard was not impressed. "If this is your answer to our problem," said one, "we'll take our choir to another church."

"Not so fast," said the Piper. He pulled a synthesizer from his roadcase and played the same song with the beautiful sounds of a pipe organ. The music filled the study and could not be contained by the massive sanctuary. Hymn lovers were overcome with the majesty of the sound and thanked the Piper profusely. Some even thought of clapping but restrained themselves.

The Piper then set up music workshops and trained the most talented youngsters in the arts of writing and composing. It wasn't long before they were taking texts from established hymns and singing new songs.

For the choir, the Piper brought out original manuscripts of the classics. They sang with great fervor and enjoyed the Piper's knowledge of their kind of music.

When the Piper finished his final seminar, he asked for payment. Unfortunately, he did this the first Sunday of combined contemporary and traditional worship.

"Payment?" screamed the choir director. "You have ruined our service! Certainly you have appeased the younger generation with their guitars and gospel songs, but you have done something far worse. You have legitimized their musical form. We will not give you a penny."

"I am not in the mood to dicker," the Piper said. "I've been called by a prominent science periodical to rid them of some pesky creationists. It's time to pay the Piper. You won't like what happens if you don't."

"We do appreciate all you've done here," said the pastor in a conciliatory tone. "But I think we'll handle things ourselves from now on. We've invited a boomer specialist to come in next week and straighten out the kids."

"Then you leave me no alternative," said the Piper. He pulled a strange machine from his case and turned it on. A loud buzz filled the church, and the congregation looked in amazement as hymnals and sheet music disappeared. Guitars, synthesizers and even the massive pipe organ were sucked into the machine, never to be heard again.

In addition, each member lost the ability to distinguish one note from another. On that day not one person could sing a tune or even hum in the shower. Songbirds around the church flew from their nests, and the halls fell silent.

The Piper took his machine to the river and pitched all the notes and chords, all the time signatures, the instruments, the choir robes and the piano into the deep stream.

"You have no right to take our music away," said one choir member in a rather monotone voice. "If we'd known you were going to do this we would gladly have sung a praise chorus or two."

"That's right," agreed a baby boomer. "And we would sing some of those old hymns if we could have our music back. They weren't that bad."

But it was too late. As much as the congregation wished for another chance, the Piper had taken their music from them forever.

There remains one ray of hope for First Church, however. If you listen closely, among the shaking rattles and chimes of mobiles, you may hear the faintest strains of "Jesus Loves Me" coming from the nursery.

KING MIDAS &
THE CHRISTIAN TOUCH

ome time ago there lived a king named Midas who was very wealthy and quite concerned about the encroachment of the pluralistic society on his kingdom. He spent much of his time fighting for prayer in the schools. Curiously, however, he very seldom prayed with his lovely daughter, Christiana.

While the hot sun beat down in the afternoon, Christiana would play in the vineyard while King Midas thought about ways to reverse the culture's dreadful trend toward secularism.

"Please read to me," said Christiana one day. She loved to hear Mother Goose rhymes, and because the king could not think of a Christian alternative, he took up the book and recited "Jack and Jill."

At the part where Jack fell down, a thought came to him: *If only everything in my kingdom could become Christian, the world would be a much better place. The world would be safe for my daughter, and I wouldn't have to worry about lawsuits, unless of course it was a Christian world that didn't read the Bible very carefully.*

"If only I could have the power to make everything Christian," he said aloud. "I would give anything to have that power, anything at all."

As he stared into space as fathers sometimes do, Christiana said, "Come on, Dad, read!"

But her pleas fell on deaf ears, for all at once King Midas was stunned by a bright light and a piercing voice that said, "Your wish has been granted, King Midas. As soon as the sun rises tomorrow, anything you touch will become Christian."

"Will it change into a deeply committed Christian thing or simply become lukewarm?" King Midas asked.

"That is for you to see," said the voice—which being interpreted means, "It's for me to know and you to find out."

And find out he did. In the morning King Midas awoke fitfully from sleep and found the mattress he was lying on had become Christian. The tag displayed the manufacturer's name with addresses in Wheaton, Illinois, and Colorado Springs, Colorado.

Anything I touch now will become Christian, thought the king. *How wonderful for me and all my kingdom.*

Immediately he jumped out of bed and put on his shoes, which became sandals. He ran down the stairway eagerly, looking for objects to touch, and came upon his daughter's book of nursery rhymes. One touch, and instantly the book was transformed! Every story, every poem, now had a religious slant.

The king ran on to one of his favorite places, the royal baseball diamond. Players for the minor-league Nuggets were running wind sprints and chewing tobacco, which should be done only by professionals.

Forgetting his gift, King Midas approached a particularly rugged player who was the star of the team. Upon seeing the king the slugger uttered a few unprintable words and offered his hand.

Instantly the chaw in his cheek and his stubbly beard disappeared. "Praise the Lord," he said to the king. "It's a real blessing to meet you."

I've never heard this player talk this way in postgame interviews, the king thought. Aloud he said, "You are certainly a talented young man."

"Well, I just want to thank the good Lord," the player said.

King Midas was overjoyed about the effect he was having on his kingdom. He ran into a royal used-car lot and leaned against one of the automobiles to catch his breath. Straightaway, each end of the car was graced with bumper stickers that said "One Way" and "Honk If You Love Jesus."

King Midas then stepped into the dealer's office and shook hands with the owner and his sales staff. They too turned Christian and began praising the Lord by offering markdowns on their inventory.

The king walked by the royal broadcasting center with its radio and television outlets and thought, *Why not?* Thus it came to be that one minute his kingdom was watching a talk show that paraded people with every known relational dysfunction across the screen. The next minute they were watching the same people being counseled by a Christian psychologist/faith healer.

King Midas was not only delighted in the change, he was ecstatic that all he had to do was touch a person or object to make it holy. No hard work, no prayer, no long days of waiting and struggling. Just a little touch, and each thing or person was converted.

Walking back toward the palace, he touched flowers and trees, which thereupon sprouted "Jesus Loves Me" buds. He met the gardener, an unkempt, bushy-haired individual with a long beard. When King Midas touched him, his hair turned three different shades of orange, and he went running toward the nearest televised sporting event to hold up a "John 3:16" sign.

The king approached two children who were playing with violent action toys. One touch, and the toys became biblical violent action toys with spears and slingshots.

A group of concerned politicians had gathered by the palace. When King Midas shook hands with them, they turned from the opposition party to the "League of Believers," a new Christian coalition.

King Midas knew he had one important person left to touch. He found Christiana alone by the grapevines, reading her new Mother Goose book. He touched her gently on the cheek and watched closely to observe the metamorphosis.

To his surprise, he did not see any change. So he touched her shoulder a bit more firmly.

"What are you doing, Father?" she asked.

"I'm trying to turn you into a Christian," he said, and grabbed her arm and shook it vigorously.

"Father," she said meekly, "since my youth I have known of the things of God, as the Sunday-school teachers have taught me. The words from the book about the man from Galilee, his perfect life, his perfect sacrifice and the forgiveness he offers—that message touched my heart long ago."

"Then I have been misled," said the king. "I have thought all this time that I was making a society Christian. But you are saying it is not true. The voice I heard must have been lying."

"The only One who can truly change our culture and the people in it is the One who touches the heart," Christiana said with wisdom beyond her years. "You certainly have affected the outward appearance of men, such as the baseball player and the used-car salesman. But tomorrow one will put cork in his bat and the other will overcharge his customers for a brake job unless the Spirit reaches them."

King Midas looked sad, and teardrops fell down his cheeks like so many little fish symbols. He loved his daughter even more because of the valuable lesson he had learned.

From that day forward he and Christiana devoted themselves to prayer for the kingdom. They regularly visited the poor, the widows and the orphans and set up a shelter for the homeless. They related the timeless message that the Great King of Glory loves people and wants them to know him. One by one people's lives were changed, and the kingdom was never the same.

THE 77 HABITS OF HIGHLY INEFFECTIVE CHRISTIANS

*An ineffective Christian
never remembers to thank anyone
under any circumstances.
Might as well learn that before
you begin this book.*

PREFACE

Not long ago I decided to take a break from all the conferences on excellence and spiritual success. I had been to seminars and dinners and week-long meetings that exhausted every conceivable topic concerning the Christian life. I went to men's meetings, couples' retreats, leadership training and Bible walk-throughs. I gathered countless notebooks and heard speakers who encouraged biblical success in business and life. I attended sports banquets featuring born-again athletes and coaches. To be honest, I was looking for a meeting whose title did not have the number 7 in it, something less stressful and frankly, not so spiritual.

Quite by accident I stumbled into a symposium called "The Quest for Mediocrity: A Modern Spiritual Paradigm." It was held in the ballroom of a seedy little hotel near Chicago. The carpeting was burnt orange, and the years of serving pressed chicken dinners had left a discernible pallor in the room. The speaker that day was Dr. Virgil Lacking, Professor of Lethargy in the Department of Indifference at Southwest Complacent State. It came as no surprise that his doctorate was honorary.

I found Dr. Lacking's approach so refreshing, so liberating to my soul, that during a break for lukewarm coffee I approached him and proposed this volume. Though he believed it to be a good idea, his penchant for languor caused frequent manuscript delays.

As the months dragged by in frustration, I decided to assemble this helpful volume myself using Dr. Lacking's unexceptional material. I have tried to write with his voice, with his lack of authority and with his ineffective style. The charts and artwork are reproduced from an independent recollection of his seminars. The 77 habits are adapted from notes found in wastebaskets and from a smattering of interviews Dr. Lacking gave over the years.

These 77 habits are by no means exhaustive of the many ways one may become ineffective in the Christian life, but I believe they represent the very best of the worst.

For study groups and personal enrichment, at the end of the explanation of each habit I have included questions, action points and, where applicable, Scriptures to avoid. These should aid in your quest for total spiritual impotence. There is a self-test at the end to take before and after reading so you may score your level of ineffectivity.

Of course if your desire is to be more effective in your spiritual life, if you yearn for a deeper walk with the God who made you, if you wish to live in a Christlike way with your family, friends and those around you, if you seriously desire discipleship, I suppose you could modify these habits and simply do the opposite of the advice listed here.

Whatever your desire—an average, normal, mediocre Christian life or a serious, self-denying, cross-bearing adventure—may this volume teach and spur you to the desired end.

Sola Mediocrum Ineffectum
(The misuse of Latin phrases is greatly encouraged by the author.)

Habit #
1

DICHOTOMIZE YOUR LIFE

Truly ineffective Christians apportion their lives into secular and sacred components. They view spirituality as something done on specific days at specific times for specific reasons. The rest of their existence is unaffected by the "spiritual" realm.

This lifestyle is known as compartmentalization. You must strive to see church, worship, Bible study and religious activities as inherently spiritual, while you view everything else as secular.

Don't miss this opportunity to frolic in mediocrity. If you talk about your faith at work, if you memorize or read Scripture at times other than those prescribed for a religious interlude, or if you even think about spiritual themes during the secular compartment of life, you are not being ineffective.

If you see a beautiful sunrise while driving in your car pool, resist the urge to talk about the beauty of creation and the creativity of God—particularly if there are those in the car who believe in evolution. Never reference the other aspect of your compartmentalized life.

It is totally acceptable to pray, silently of course, about big work decisions, a pay raise or relational difficulties. This will make you feel like you're bringing yourself to the Almighty. However, you must squelch the urge to bring the smaller things to him, the everyday, mundane things. This would cause you to believe God is interested in all aspects of life. To be ineffective you must keep him at bay, distant from the totality of your existence.

Remember, your life is not something whole to present to God, only parts you control.

Scripture to Avoid: Romans 12:1

MAKE TOLERANCE YOUR GOD

Habit #
2

Following trends in the culture will increase your ineffectivity. Study society closely and practice assiduously the trends you see. One current destroyer of the vital Christian life is tolerance.

It should be said that tolerance can be used for good, but in today's culture it has gone to an extreme, and extremes are very good.

You must, in your tolerance, accept anything and everything. Whether the issue is homosexual rights or funding for the arts, you must convince yourself that all viewpoints are not only valid but also equal. In this way you destroy the notion that there are absolutes. Tolerance taken to its logical end helps obliterate the fact that there is such a thing as truth and that we are bound to it and not our opinion polls.

Tolerate sin. Tolerate divergent opinion. Tolerate films that rewrite history. Tolerate perversion. Tolerate Elvis impersonators, if you possibly can.

In this resolve of accepting others no matter what they say or believe, you should perceive yourself as living a Christlike life, thereby confusing tolerance with love. You will then become popular with news organizations that look for sane, tolerant folks to juxtapose to the narrow-minded religious sorts who just don't want people to have any fun. If you get really good at it, you might run for public office.

Remember, society esteems tolerance for everything—except for those who hold to absolutes. They are intolerant, selfish and puritanical little sniveling . . . well, you get the point.

For Further Thought: What have you tolerated in others that goes against Christianity? What else could you tolerate that you haven't already?

LIVE IN THE CIRCLE OF INEFFECTIVITY

Crucial to the idea of spiritual squalor is the circle of ineffectivity. You see this lifestyle diagrammed below.

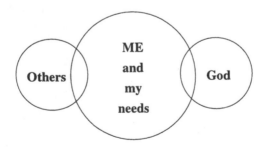

To live as ineffective as possible, put at the center of your life "Me and My Needs." This must always be paramount. You must never consider anything in any way other than how it will affect "Me and My Needs."

A Christian living a dynamic Christian life would, of course, have God as the center circle with "Me" being the smallest. You, however, must keep God to the side and make the spheres converge as little as possible, preferably on Sunday mornings or in emergency situations, such as when your flight takes a two-thousand-foot plunge while you're eating a fruit cup.

Likewise, keep "Others" outside your circle. The way you treat others shows how much you love God. The farther away you keep them, the farther you will be from him and the more ineffective you'll be.

Ineffective Exercise: Diagram your life with the above circles. Which is the largest? Do the circles intersect at all? Do you even need the other two circles? Discuss.

Habit #

4

NEVER BE CONTENT

Effective Christians are content, so you must strive for discontented living. Being content means achieving a certain state of peace with one's circumstances. Satisfaction. An ineffective Christian must never be satisfied.

On the physical level, you must not be content with your appearance. Lament your large nose, your thin lips and the gap between your teeth. Pine for a bigger brain or broader shoulders and do not focus on God's unique creation that is you.

Materially, you must not be content with your station in life. Always look at those who have more and condemn them for it. Thankfully, most Christians in the West are by nature discontent.

One of the key secrets to ineffective Christian living is an inner desire for more. It rips at the heart every waking moment. Make it yours. It doesn't matter what that "more" is. It could be a minivan with cup holders or a refrigerator with an ice-cube/fudge maker. It could even be something spiritual. I know many ineffective Christians who say they desire the "deeper life" but really want to see an angel by the expressway. They simply lack contentment with the spiritual experiences God has given them.

Be sure to cloak your lack of contentment in the shroud of excellence. Justify the never-ending search to fill the void of self by "aiming higher." We know the goal for much of this talk is simply self-gratification and indulgence. We work longer hours to make more money to buy more things that don't deliver, and we call this excellence.

Make discontent a part of your everyday life and you will become more and more ineffective.

Scripture to Avoid: Hebrews 13:5

SHUN PAIN

Habit #
5

If you are a Christian, it is inevitable that you will experience hardship and difficulty. Ineffective believers have learned the careful art of shunning pain.

In his infinite wisdom, the God of the universe puts pain in the path of his creatures. This draws them closer to him, causes them to rely on his strength and not their own, and helps them focus on heaven, where there will be no more pain.

Ineffective Christian living seeks to soothe and salve pain through artificial means. You may think that drugs and alcohol are the only ways to do this, but modern society has infinitely more resources. You can escape pain by watching television, listening to music, pouring yourself into your work or even getting involved in "religious" activities.

A physical problem is usually diagnosed when there is recurring pain. The malady can then be treated by a physician. Likewise, spiritual problems often come to the surface through the painful circumstances of life. If you simply ignore that pain, you will continually stunt your spiritual growth and thereby reach a higher plain of ineffectivity.

This is also true of others' pain. When someone else is hurting, this may cause a certain amount of identification for you. Do not allow them to pull you into this vicious cycle, because another person's pain can often cause you to analyze yourself. Simply say you'll be praying for them and watch a video or take a nap.

For whatever reason, pain seems to produce perseverance and a stronger faith in committed Christians. But for you, avoidance is the best method.

Ineffective Exercise: In order not to think of something painful in your past and how it has deepened your walk with God, write your own ineffective catchphrase such as "Shun Pain, Shun Gain." Repeat as often as necessary.

Habit #

6

BASE YOUR FAITH SOLELY ON FEELINGS & EXPERIENCE

How do you know you are a Christian? For ineffective believers, the answer changes from day to day.

It is important to base your spiritual condition not on the finished work of Christ, but on feelings and experience.

If you have a relative who was near death on the operating table but saw a white light from the Great Beyond, use this as your proof of the afterlife. Base your salvation on any dream you have, particularly when you eat a pepperoni, anchovy and peanut-butter pizza just before going to bed.

Listen for the still, small voice that comes from a can of tuna. Watch for a sign from God in the lottery numbers.

You'll make much less of an impact on the world if you base your spirituality on feelings. One day you should fly high about the goodness of God over a recent raise. The next day be depressed because you need a new carburetor. This is part of the ebb and flow of an ineffective Christian. You're sure of God's love one day, confused the next.

Do not cultivate a depth to your Christian life. Instead seek warm fuzzy feelings toward God. Purchase a guitar and learn "Pass It On." Be prepared to smash the instrument when you mess up the Dm_7 chord toward the end. Always say you believe the Bible, but trust in your experience and feelings.

Question to Ponder: What happened to you today that let you know you're a Christian or not a Christian?

Habit #

7

MAKE PRAYER OCCASIONAL

Communication is one of the most important aspects of any relationship, and that is why you should make prayer something occasional in your life.

If you were to see your union with God as something vital and living, you would desire constant communication. After all, to know you can speak to the King of Kings at a moment's notice is truly a staggering thought.

But ineffective Christian living will make this communication sporadic, or simply an option that's tacked on at dinner and during worship services.

As I've said earlier in this volume, you should pray only about the large decisions in life, like who to marry, what college to attend and whether to get tinted glass in your minivan. But true mediocrity demands even less. What you must actually do is make up your mind about the decision that faces you, and then subtly conform the will of the Almighty to your own. This not only justifies whatever choice you make but also makes you feel spiritual since you can rightly say, "I prayed about it."

Prayer should be something that comes not from the heart but from the head. You must pray the same things, the same phrases over and over, for this will make you more comfortable, and comfort is always the goal of the ineffective Christian. During the worship service it is fine to bow or even kneel, but your mind must not be on the words you are praying but on the mental images of your ballgame, your dinner or the department store you could visit while the kids are in Sunday school.

Since you think about so many other things when you pray, keep your prayers short and to the point. "I want _____ and ____. In Jesus' name, Amen."

Scripture to Avoid: 1 Thessalonians 5:17
Ineffective Hymn:
"Sweet Minute of Prayer"
Sweet minute of prayer, sweet minute of
    prayer,
That's just about all that I can spare.
I have regrets and lots of sin
So I'll see if I can squeeze them in.
In sea-sons of dis-tress and grief
My greatest prayer is quick relief.
But things are swell, I've no despair,
I'll just spend half a minute in prayer.

Habit #

MAJOR ON THE MINORS

Since the whole topic of faith is so nebulous, so hard to grasp, the ineffective Christian must choose two or three issues and cling to them ferociously. While this clinging does very little for your spirituality, it will make you feel like a Christian, and feelings are everything when you want to be ineffective.

You must focus your daily gaze on these chosen points, rather than on God's grace and the whole counsel of his Word. The subjects you identify with not only will make you feel like a righteous person but also will help you judge others.

For example, focus your faith on the rapture and the end times. Or home schooling. Or tongues. Women must submit to wearing dresses with small floral prints on every odd-numbered Sunday.

What you choose as your issue is not as important as how tightly you hold to it. Of course you cannot use as your points specific scriptural verities like the sinlessness of Christ, the virgin birth or the resurrection. You must choose something obscure enough in Scripture that there is disagreement in the body. This will further divide believers and keep them fighting among themselves rather than making an impact on the world, so you've not only kept yourself ineffective but spread the mediocrity around.

Discussion Question: What is the litmus test by which you judge another person's Christianity? Choose now if you don't have one:

1. Age of earth
2. Author of Hebrews
3. Age of author of Hebrews
4. Location of Noah's ark
5. Type of fruit eaten in the Garden of Eden
6. Moses' sandal size

Habit #

STRIVE FOR IMBALANCE

You must go one step further if you desire the ineffective Christian life. Simply put, you should strive for an uneven keel. Live off balance. Your ship of faith must continually list.

This means you don't stop at majoring on the minors. Continue to practice unbalanced living at every turn.

Focus on your family so much that both parents quit working. Decide you can't really be good parents if you don't spend every waking moment of the day protecting your children and training them. Or become so involved in work and career that you forget you even have children.

Read only fiction. Lose yourself in a fantasy world of made-up Christian characters who fight angels or move west. Or get lost in the world of the "real." People who think only nonfiction can be "true" live dreadfully uncreative lives.

Do not take Scripture as a whole, comparing verses and passages. Treat each phrase independently from the rest. This will allow you, for example, to justify your "prayer only" method of healing by a passage in James when God has provided a perfectly good shot of penicillin from the HMO you declined at the office.

Imbalanced living will further marginalize you from the rest of the world. By going overboard you can take even something that was created good and turn it into a tool for ineffectivity.

Question to Ponder: In what ways are you living an unbalanced life today? How can you make your ship of faith list further?

BE A HEARER ONLY

Habit #

10

It may surprise you that some of the most ineffective Christians today learn more about the Bible than anyone else. Let me explain.

Those who constantly sit under the teaching of the Word have a wonderful opportunity for mediocrity. These are people who most likely have five or more Bibles as well as a shelf of Christian books and commentaries, and say "Amen" while listening to their Christian radio station (with all car windows down, volume up). These people teach classes, answer questions correctly and pray an inordinately long time on Wednesday evening.

But the pivotal word for them is *hear,* for they only listen to the Word and don't do it in their lives. Follow their example. Become filled with the desire to hear facts and view charts and maps about the Bible so you can tell others all the neat information you've gleaned.

But do not *do* the Word. Go away from each conference or seminar feeling very good about transcribing the entire outline and all the scriptural references, but don't do a thing about changing your own life.

If you encounter an admonition against a particular sin, simply look past the passage until you come to something you're already doing right. This, of course, is like a man who looks in the mirror at a restaurant and fails to remove the broccoli lodged between his teeth, but is quick to point out the creamed corn on his neighbor's lapel.

Hear as much about Christianity as you can, but do as little as possible so it will have the least effect in your own life.

Scripture to Avoid: James 1:23-25

Habit #

11

BE A SPIRITUAL SPONGE

There is another component to "hearing" the Word that will make you even more ineffective. As stated, some hear the Word and do nothing about their own life. But spiritual sponges provide an alternate means to mediocrity.

Spiritual sponges, like the hearer, show up at every service, take notes on sermons, memorize verses, attend retreats, buy Christian books galore and subscribe to every Christian magazine and devotional.

Spiritual sponges know all the kings of the Old Testament. In alphabetical order. Spiritual sponges know the diet of the prophets, how many calories are in a locust and how much the ark would cost today if built with original materials. Spiritual sponges desire the true trivia of the Word.

Unlike "hearers," spiritual sponges are open to correction and will change sinful habits and behaviors in their lives. What spiritual sponges do not do is use their knowledge to help others. They will not teach a class. They will not present themselves for leadership in the church. They won't drive a bus or take the offering, and most of all, they will not engage anyone outside the church in meaningful conversation regarding what they know.

Call them shy, call them intellectual, call them introspective. Just don't call on them to pray out loud during a service. If you must learn more about the Bible and the Christian life, make sure you imitate the spiritual sponge, and you will be filled with lots of knowledge but empty of concern for others.

Action Point: What bit of biblical knowledge that could change a life can you keep to yourself today?

Habit #

12

PROVOKE YOUR CHILDREN TO WRATH

One of the great ways to display a defective faith is the way you treat your children. Everyone knows how vexing it is for the little termites to see your inconsistency lived out before them. The good news is, you can do even more damage.

Provoke them. Poke them with your words. Never let them feel they are accepted or that the job they do is good enough.

If, when they are young, they are told to make their beds, tell them they did a fine job while you quickly tuck and fluff. This lets them know their effort just wasn't up to your standards.

Find the one patch of grass they didn't cut. Criticize their best friend with the squirrel-tooth earring. Focus on the B in math. Make fun of their favorite music group and say, "They sound like a bunch of mistreated laboratory animals."

Start your sentences with the phrase "When I was your age . . ." Never, under any circumstances, apologize or admit you are wrong in their presence.

Above all, do not treat them as the unique beings God created them to be, but make them conform to your tastes, your desires and preferences. This will smother creativity and mold them to your likeness rather than the heavenly Father's.

Vex them to the point that they clench their teeth and run screaming to their rooms once each day, then reassure yourself that this treatment builds character. Remember, an ineffective parent can make anything seem right.

Question to Ponder: How were you provoked to wrath as a child? In what ways can you replicate that behavior today?

Habit #

13

BE THANKLESS

In all my years of analyzing truly ineffective Christians, I have yet to find one who has been thankful for anything. This is a hallmark of spiritual inadequacy.

If you were to sit down right now and list the blessings in your life, no matter what circumstance you are in, you would no doubt need reams of paper and a stack of pencils. This is why I say never, ever sit down and list the blessings in your life. It can only lead to thankfulness, which you must spurn.

Do not be thankful for God's faithfulness. If you see a miraculous answer to prayer, quickly forget it. Do not record it or tell others about God's goodness.

Do not be thankful for current material blessings like a roof over your head and food on the table. Do not compare yourself with those in the world who do not have such blessings. Instead compare yourself with the few who have bigger dwellings with better furniture and more attic space.

Do not be thankful for your spiritual blessings. Do not be thankful for God's Word, but whine that you would rather live in Old Testament days when you could hear the audible voice of God.

If you are single, desire a spouse and do not be thankful for the freedom you have. If you are married, pine for singleness and do not be thankful for the provision God has given you.

Remember, it is much easier to keep the fire of thanklessness going when you stoke it with an attitude of ingratitude.

Action Point: Make a list of the things you're not thankful for today and share them with a friend.

Ineffective Hymn:

"Count Your Problems"

When upon life's pillows you are lying down,
When you are in comfort and without a frown,
Add up all the negatives you think you see,
And you'll be surprised at just how mad you'll be.
Count your problems, name them one by one.
Count your problems, scorn what God has done.
Count your many problems, make the list real
    long.
Count your many problems while you sing this
    song.

Habit #

14

GET TO THE HEAD TABLE

If you are serious about being an ineffective Christian, you must seek to be served.

Others no doubt are under the faulty assumption that you are their equal. At every turn you must show others how important you really are. Desire to be at the head table with the important people. At work, let others know you were the one who came up with the good idea first. When it is time to clean the bathroom or scrape the mashed peas from the kitchen floor, have your spouse or children do it. This lets them know you are much more important.

Seek the up-front positions in church so that those in the congregation will know how truly gifted you are. Never seek a job like setting up chairs or scraping the dried Cheerios from the nursery floor. These carry no glory, and your efforts may go unnoticed or unrewarded. An ineffective Christian always strives for recognition.

Do not become a follower or a disciple. You must show people you desire to lead and will not be satisfied with any lesser role.

Seek applause. Gravitate to the spotlight. Use every opportunity to let others know they should bow down to you. And when they do applaud and praise your abilities with fervor, wave them off and eschew their worship. This will cause others to see you as a truly humble person and will give them even more reason to serve you.

Question to Ponder: In what ways have I sought to be served in the last week? How can I be better served? Who can I get to scrape peas today? Why are there so many Cheerios in the nursery anyway?

Habit #

15

LIVE AN UNEXAMINED LIFE

You will enter a new sphere of ineffectivity if you live life un-examined. For maximum ef-fect, stop all analysis of your relationship with your Creator. This can be achieved in a number of ways.

First, busy yourself. Keep yourself so busy you don't have time to think about life's purpose, the eternal destiny of those around you and what legacy you'll leave behind. Shut out all thoughts of the brevity of life. If someone talks about death, change the subject to more "positive" things. Never discuss the afterlife. Live for the moment, not eternity.

Second, the greatest companion of a busy life is a crowded life. Crowd it with friendly chatter and talk of the weather and how it seems to be much colder this year than last. Crowd your life with scheduled events that keep you moving from one to the other until you are living on automatic.

Third, resist the temptation to look at your motives, the "why" of what you do. Live as if you cleared that up years ago. You will become shallow, which is the byproduct of a busy life.

To live unexamined means each time a thought enters your mind about the cross, the crucified life, whether you're making your own comfort and security your god, you must immediately push it out.

Honestly, dwelling on this chapter much longer is not a good idea. Go out there and live. Be happy. Fulfill yourself. And for mediocrity's sake, stop thinking about it!

Scripture to Avoid: Psalm 139:23

Habit #
16

AVOID CLOSE RELATIONSHIPS

If you were to skip all the other habits found in this volume and cultivate only this one, you would still be classified as "highly ineffective," so avoid close relationships.

Those who would be lukewarm in their faith must keep others at a distance. Do not confess your sin to another person. Never divulge your deepest thoughts and longings. Do not open up or let yourself be the recipient of such talk. Never be there for another person, for you may be strangely drawn to the growth it produces.

If you would have lots of surface relationships, you must learn to say, "Hi, how's it goin'?" and not ever actually mean it. You should only mean *I am saying a polite hello to you so that I can move on to some other surface relationship very quickly, so please just say "Fine, how are you?" and I'll be on my way.*

Of course God wants you to have deep relationships on the horizontal plane (with people) so that you can deepen your relationship with him on the vertical plane. He often puts people in your life to knock off the rough edges. God confronts you with others and uses you to confront. He loves you with other people and uses them in your life.

My best advice is to just avoid people as much as possible.

Questions to Ponder: Who on earth knows you best and desires a closer relationship with you? Do not return their phone call. Distance yourself from this person today.

Habit # 17

TREAT GOD LIKE A PAL

Almighty. Omnipotent. The Great I Am. Awesome Lord.

These are terms you must not use or think about if you are to maximize your ineffectivity. Do not exalt God as Lord over all in your life. Instead you must bring him down to your own level. You must think of God as your heavenly pal.

The Good Lord. The man upstairs. My Big Buddy. Mr. Jesus.

You must take the gospel song "What a Friend We Have in Jesus" to the extreme. When you are tempted to sin, do not picture God sitting on his throne, surrounded by worshiping angels and beings too wonderful to describe. Do not picture him in his blinding righteousness, or yourself filled with awe as you shrink from his presence.

Picture him in a cardigan and jeans, putting his arm around you and saying, "Hey, that's okay, bud. Don't sweat the little sins, I'll take care of it." By doing this you will treat the sacrifice he made on the cross as something one business partner would do for another.

Think of God as a loving, doting grandfather, complete with rocking chair and beard. Pray casually, and without reverence, beginning your prayers with something like "Hi God, it's me."

If you focus your mind on making the Almighty, Omnipotent Master of the Universe seem like any other person, you will be well on your way to a wonderfully ineffective life.

Introspection Corner: How have you treated the Big Guy like a pal this week?

Habit #

SQUELCH "THE DREAM"

To be ineffective, you must strive for stagnant living. One of the best ways to accomplish this is to quell all efforts at "the dream."

I define "the dream" as your God-given, nagging sense of purpose. For some it is writing, for others the dream is becoming a pastor or teacher or evangelist, and for others it is simply getting the kids dressed and to church on time, though this is more "the wish" than "the dream" in our house.

"The dream" keeps coming back to you, as if God were pushing you toward an ultimate goal. No matter what you do you can't stop thinking about it: starting a ministry to a specific group, beginning an outreach to neighbors, or starting your own business to spend more time with the family.

You must fight these little whispers from the Almighty. You must tell yourself that it probably wouldn't work and nobody would come or it would cost too much money.

Keep "the dream" to yourself, because verbalizing it, even to the closest ones around you, can be deadly. They might think it a perfectly good idea and encourage you. If you do let it out, make sure you surround yourself with those whose spiritual gift is discouragement. Embrace those who will laugh and tell you how silly it is for someone like you to have such thoughts.

To live ineffectively, kill your dreams one by one, and you will be a slow-moving stream filled with stagnant water.

Action Point: Write your dream on a piece of paper and tear it into tiny bits. Repeat as often as necessary until you can't remember what it was.

Habit #

19

BE NEGATIVE

Some Christians seem to always see the glass half full, find the silver lining behind every dark cloud and make lemonade from life's lemons.

If you want to be ineffective, you must get far away from these people and seek to live negatively.

You may think I am talking about the obvious ways to demonstrate a negative attitude. Believe me, there are a million small avenues to help spread dread every day.

First, the weather. Complain that it's either too hot or too cold, too wet or too dry. If you go through a snowy winter with little sun, complain about it. Then on the first really warm day of spring tell others how hot you are.

A negative attitude starts with things you can't change such as the weather, your spouse and your children, and moves to things you can change such as your lawn, your breath and your grade point average. Half the fun of being a negative person is pointing out the flaw in things you could actually change. Because of your stubbornness or laziness, you don't, and that's great.

A negative attitude begins in the morning, when you first awaken to the new day. If there is any part of you, deep inside, that smiles at the opportunities that are ahead, you must immediately focus on how early it is or how late you are or how awful you look or how much weight you ought to lose.

Being negative is only a thought away, and it's a great avenue that connects you with the ineffective highway.

Nega-Quiz: On a scale of 1 to 10, how negative are you? Support your answer with examples. Ask others how you might be more negative today. Complain about the length of this quiz to a friend.

Habit #

20

SEEK THE QUICK, SELF-HELP SOLUTION

If you've been a Christian for any amount of time, you know life can be very difficult. For some reason God does not take rough situations from you but seems to add problems. The ineffective Christian, in those days of tumult, will seek to alleviate the difficulty with books and radio call-ins that promise a ten-step solution.

The following is my own four-step solution as an example:

Step 1. Recognize you have a problem and start looking for anyone with easy answers. The first person or book that promises a painless outcome should be trusted—or for those with financial problems, the cheapest seminar.

Step 2. Find someone who will give specific directions to alleviate your problem. These guidelines should not be nebulous like "Pray about it" or "Consider what Scripture has to say on the subject." Rather, they should be quite pointed, like "Declare bankruptcy now" or "Throw your teenager into the street tonight."

Step 3. Make your decision without consulting any trusted friends who know and care for you. People like this only get in the way and have a tendency to drag the problem out for days and even weeks.

Step 4. Trust your instincts. After you've made your rash decision, lean on your own understanding. Remember, God loves those who self-help themselves.

Christians who seek to make life easy will be the most ineffective in the long run. The rule of thumb is, seek a solution, not God.

Introspection Corner: Describe a time in your life when you didn't seek quick answers. How would you be different today had you followed a ten-step process?

Habit #
21

LIVE A HOMOGENIZED FAITH

It is pivotal that you seek stunted spiritual growth to keep your ineffectivity at a maximum level. One way to accomplish this is to live "homogenized." By this I mean you must only drink in the milk of the Word.

Learn John 3:16 and be able to recite it clearly, but have no idea what the surrounding verses say or what context it's in. If someone asks a tough theological question on an unrelated subject, respond, "Well, John 3:16 says . . ." Make John 3:16 the exclusive passage of your life that answers everything, and always recite it with a vacant smile.

Demand a Bible with lots of pictures in it. Focus on the chapters that are illustrated with the most vibrant colors.

At times you will be challenged to look at other parts of Scripture and think. As much as it lies within you, daydream. Think of love and harps and clouds and all the fun you'll have in heaven. But if you must read, emphasize the love of God in those passages and skip over the attributes of righteousness or holiness or justice.

If you saturate yourself with milk at the exclusion of meat, you will remain childish in your faith and make a very small impression on the world.

Verse to Read: 1 Peter 2:2a. Read the first part of the verse, then draw a picture of God's love with the crayon of your choice. (Remember to use the whole page and try to color in the lines.)

Habit # 22

MAKE MUSIC THE BIG ISSUE

As stated earlier, the unexceptional believer finds one issue and bases their life calling on it. Because music is so controversial, there is no better focus.

Music can stir the soul. It can explain theological truths and plumb the depths of subjects like grace, mercy and the grandeur of God. Ineffective Christians take this wonderful gift and use it to divide.

Some may advocate singing only hymns written before 1800. Others will further segment the hymnal and insist on up-tempo tunes like "He Lives" and "Wonderful Grace of Jesus" in the morning service and "Like a River Glorious" in the evening. Another person may threaten to leave the congregation if you don't sing "In the Garden" at least once a quarter.

On the other side are those who enjoy praise choruses or the latest worship tunes they learned at weekend conferences. Your favorites should include particularly repetitive songs like "Sing Alleluia" or those that change only a few words like "Alleluia."

It is imperative that you not in any way seek a balance between these two extremes. You must not appreciate differing styles of music, different instruments or ways of expressing praise. Stay narrow. Stay focused.

Do not quibble over the words of the text; this actually shows signs of maturity and that you're analyzing what you're singing. Instead base your musical taste only on style. This ensures discord in the body and ineffective living for you.

For Further Reflection: Take a moment and sing through the hymn that follows.

"Hymn for the Ineffective Christian"
(sung to the tune "Nettleton," or "Come, Thou Fount")
Come, thou Fount of ev'ry blessing,
Give me what I want today;
Entertainment never ceasing,
Paths of comfort line my way.
Teach me nothing that will make me grow,
I want to stay right where I am;
True meat comes from your Word, I know,
But I crave spiritual SPAM.

I try hard to lead a good life,
I recycle, clean my feet.
I buy presents for my good wife,
Help old ladies cross the street.
I have quit my game of poker
And I'm trusting you'll be glad.
My life is so mediocre,
But I'm really not that bad.

O to self how much I'm focused,
Daily I'm constrained to be!
You give manna, I choose locust,
And the world revolves 'round me.
Prone to squander love, so infinite,
To forget my loving Lord.
Take an hour, no, take two minutes,
That's all that I can afford.

"Chorus of Mediocrity" (sung to "Alleluia")
In-ef-fect-ive   (8 times)
Living for self   (8 times)
Meet my needs now   (8 times)
Make me hap-py   (8 times)
In-ef-fect-ive   (8 times)

Habit #
23

CULTIVATE WORRY

Cultivate worry like a garden. To be fully ineffective you must till the soil of worry and plant seeds of angst. Angst will take root and bring forth fear, which is simply worry on steroids.

You must worry about the little things of life. Will there be enough antifreeze for the car? Will your aluminum siding last a full twenty years? Worry about choices. Which dinner to make. Which bank to choose. What toaster to buy. Which professor to take for pivotal courses such as "Medieval Indo-European Macramé Patterns" or "The Influence of *Gilligan's Island* on Greco-Roman Mud Wrestling." Worry about making mistakes, even when all options available are good ones.

You must worry particularly about things you have virtually no control over. Let worry control you, vex you and hound your every step. If you have a difficult task, do not spend time planning; simply worry, and spread it to those around you.

Never pray about the object of your worry, because this might cause you to put things in perspective. Do not reflect on the awesome God you serve.

Do not learn from your past. It's probably true that the very thing you're worrying about has some correlation to a worry you've experienced before that turned out to be nothing to worry about. Resist the temptation to remember, and thus continue worrying.

Above all, do not exercise faith, because faith is the antithesis of anxiety. Focus on yourself, for this is the raison d'être of worry. (Worry about spelling *raison d'etre* correctly as well.)

If you're concerned that you are not as ineffective as you should be after reading this book, follow my advice and worry about it.

Scriptures to Avoid: Philippians 4:6; Matthew 6:25-34

Habit # 24

BE A HIGH-MAINTENANCE BELIEVER

One way to be ineffective and stay that way is to live a high-maintenance Christianity. This works well in your relationship to God and others.

By "high-maintenance" I mean that you cannot do anything independently. You constantly are looking to God and others for help and direction in areas that really need no clarification. Every detail of life has to be mapped out and signed in triplicate before you act.

In your relationship to others at church you must expect unbelievable levels of communication. You should always have a question about the music chosen by the choir. You should always raise your hand in Sunday school and harp on the typeface the office staff chose for the bulletin.

A cursory look at the high-maintenance Christian might lead you to believe they really are dependent upon God because they seem to consult him at every turn. In truth, people in this category are not really concerned about what God wants from them. Rather, they veil their own desires in continual clarifications so that in the end they get their own way.

Being high-maintenance can lead you to new levels of ineffectivity as you require more and more people to meet your every need. Remember, the more you make others center around you (refer to circle of ineffectivity on page 13), the more ineffective you become as a follower of Christ.

For Further Reflection: How have you been high-maintenance today? Call five people right now and ask their opinion. In what ways can you become more centered on self?

Habit #

VIEW PEOPLE AS CONVERTS

Even a casual Christian takes the Great Commission seriously. However, you can thwart any good intentions you have in this realm by treating people simply as potential converts.

The worst possible thing you can do in evangelism is to think of people as individuals, made in the image of God, loved by their Creator. Do not think of them as people for whom Christ died. Think of them as notches on your religious revolver.

You must cultivate a cavalier attitude toward the whole idea of "sharing your faith," and as much as possible take out the relational aspect of the task. Try to see non-Christians as a nameless, faceless mass of humanity rather than that neighbor down the street or your close relative.

Stick tracts in hotel rooms and drive-thrus, in phone booths and on windshields. Wear T-shirts that dramatically state the Christian message in a slogan, particularly if it's a rip-off of a secular advertisement. Do this not to get the message out, but to assuage your own feelings of guilt.

Mind you, there are some vibrant Christians who use tracts, T-shirts and other means to strike up conversations with unbelievers. But you must use these methods only as means to escape relationships.

Remember, the goal of evangelism for the ineffective Christian is not to bring others into the kingdom and a right relationship with God; it is to make you think you've done your duty, and ultimately to make you feel better.

For Further Thought: Think of one person who isn't a Christian you could be praying for right now. Now stop thinking about that or you won't be ineffective.

Habit #
26

EVANGELIZE STELLAR CANDIDATES

There is one exception to ineffective evangelism that should be addressed here. When you treat people like numbers, you will feel righteous for spreading the Word. To enhance this feeling you should utilize the "Stellar Candidate" approach.

Have you ever seen someone on television or in a film and wondered what it would be like if that person were to become a Christian? This is a perfectly natural thing for a believer to do, but you must take this thought to its extreme.

You must begin not only praying for the salvation of your stellar candidate—let's say the artist formerly known as "Billy-Bob"—but also writing the candidate and telling that person how much you are praying for him. Stalk Billy-Bob and convince yourself you're doing so out of Christian compassion.

Then begin telling others how much you are praying and writing Billy-Bob and how great the kingdom of God would be if only Billy-Bob would become a Christian! In this way you will plant in other minds the thought that is already full grown in your own, that God uses people with great talent and visibility in greater ways than he can ordinary, everyday people like yourself.

But by earnestly striving for the salvation of Billy-Bob, whose name you drop every few minutes, you elevate yourself above the ordinary and eventually will become known as "The Person Whose Ministry Is Praying for Billy-Bob."

Action Point: What singer, actor, politician, writer, news anchor, media mogul or billionaire would you like to be known as praying for? How much more would you pray for a celebrity than for a coworker?

Habit # 27

MONEY ISN'T ANY OF GOD'S BUSINESS

Christians who take their faith seriously know that finances are an integral part of their spiritual lives. How they use their money is a barometer of their trust in the provision of the Almighty.

But you, if you are to increase your ineffectiveness, should treat money as none of God's business. After all, it's yours, not his. You earned it, right? You should be able to spend it any way you please.

You will be tempted through onslaughts of Scriptures and Christian financial counselors to give to your church, to ministries that help you and to a variety of worthy causes. Treat these people like phone solicitors.

I have heard many committed Christians ask, "Should I tithe on the gross or after taxes?" This is entirely the wrong question. The correct question is "Why should I give at all?"

Remind yourself that God owns the cattle on a thousand hills and the riches of heaven. Compare that with the measly amount you make and you'll keep every penny.

Remember, you are setting an example before your children every week when that offering plate passes. You are letting them know how much you value the things of God, how much you trust him and wish to give back to him. If you want them to be ineffective, say you love God but palm the ten-dollar bill as the plate passes.

Ineffective Financial Exercise: Total your gross earnings for this year. Estimate your taxes. Total all your expenses. Divide the remainder by 10. Take that amount to the mall and treat yourself—you deserve it. If there's anything left over, think about giving it on Sunday.

Habit #

28

TREAT THE OLD TESTAMENT AS A STORYBOOK

Adam. Eve. Noah. Abraham. Moses. Joshua. Ruth. David. Solomon.

If you are to be ineffective as a Christian, you must treat these people as mere characters in God's little playhouse. Never, ever think of them as real humans who lived real lives.

Tell yourself it is not important whether someone like Esther actually lived in time and space. It is not important whether Abraham physically raised a knife to kill his son—I think it was Abraham, wasn't it?—or that Noah built a big boat and put all the animals on it.

What is important, you must convince yourself, is that these tales were passed from one generation to the next to emphasize a moral framework. Thus it's not important if there were really ten commandments written in stone (or that it was actual stone). The important thing is we have stories to tell children so they'll be good.

Tell yourself, and others, that because we have the New Testament it's not important to read anything before Matthew. It's not important to see the parallels between Israel and the church. It's not important to learn of the archaeological finds that match with the words of Old Testament writers.

In this way you will divorce history from the written text and, in the end, the truth spoken of in the Scriptures. Keep distance between yourself and the characters of the Old Testament, because you may see in them pictures of yourself and your own life that you don't want to see.

A *Moment to Mull:* What is your favorite Old Testament character? What actor/actress would you choose to play him/her in a movie of the week? Which director other than Oliver Stone would you choose?

Habit #

MEASURE SUCCESS BY NUMBERS

If someone asks a business executive their definition of success, the professional would no doubt point to the bottom line. How much money was made in the previous year? A farmer will point to the number of bushels of corn or head of cattle.

For you, an ineffective Christian, what is the definition of success? The answer should be numbers. The more numbers of the nameless hordes you can attract to your church, Sunday school, conference or Bible study, the more success you possess.

This means you will do just about anything outside of breaking the Ten Commandments to get people in, and sometimes it's probably okay to do that.

Conversely, those who do not have numbers are not experiencing success. Look down on such people. Perhaps there is a small church struggling to make disciples, worship God and be faithful to its calling.

Stay away from this type of place; it can only bring you closer to God.

Instead gravitate toward the large gatherings that attract numbers through artificial means. Of course there are larger ministries that seek to make disciples, worship and be faithful, and you should stay away from these as well.

With all that is in you, make numbers most important. Do not feel like you have done anything significant until you see lots of heads. Become discouraged and despair if you do not achieve the success you crave. This will thwart any real progress you may have made with those around you.

Ineffective Growth Exercise: What number would constitute success for church attendance? What number would constitute success for your yearly income? Write these two numbers down in a conspicuous place and refer to them often.

Habit #

30

BLAME OTHERS

Whenever you are confronted with your sin, whenever you feel conviction in your spirit, whenever you are tempted to take responsibility for your actions, remember the ineffective Christian always blames others.

In the marriage relationship it is best when you are caught in the wrong to begin your next sentence with "I know that, but if you hadn't . . ." This shifts the blame for your actions back onto your spouse, which is a wonderful way to escape scrutiny.

When your coworkers discover a mistake you made at work, such as putting coffee grounds in the photocopier, blame someone else. Excuse yourself by saying, "I was confused. My last employer had a coffee machine bigger than this copier, and it made copies, received faxes and e-mails, and made cappuccino."

This is a particularly important element in the process of becoming an ineffective parent. When you make a mistake, expunge the guilt by placing blame and shame on the child rather than absorbing the fault yourself.

Finally, never, ever consider uttering the phrase "I'm wrong." Just as insurance companies urge you to never say it at the scene of an accident, you should never admit anything. Also, do not say "I'm sorry," or "Please forgive me."

When you blame others constantly for your mistakes, over time you will generate the belief that the only reason you sin is because of other people, or that you don't really sin at all. When you reach this point you are at the height of ineffectivity in your Christian life.

Bumper Sticker: Have you blamed your child today?

Habit #

31

LEAVE FASTING TO THE WEIRD PEOPLE

If you want to stay in a state of languor in your faith, shun the spiritual disciplines. Shrink from any activity that puts a degree of demand on your spirit, your intellect and your body.

For example, you must never fast. Fasting should be considered something weird people do. Think of fasting as an Old Testament phenomenon or something John the Baptist would do after a week of locust casserole.

Convince yourself that going without food for a period of time would be dangerous to your health or would set a bad example before your children. Think of any excuse plausible to give those around you.

Fasting points you toward the eternal and focuses you on things above. Fasting emphasizes that your body is subject to your will, that your appetite can be controlled. Those notions just don't fit with ineffective living.

If you find people who do fast regularly, run from them. They probably pray way too often and read their Bibles every day.

If you find that you are in a position where you must fast, make a big deal about it. Walk around with a long face and drool when you see someone munching on potato chips. Moan a lot. Every chance you get you should say something like "That sandwich really looks good, but I can't have any. Fasting, you know."

For Further Reflection: What foods would you least like to give up in a fast? Make a list and keep it handy when tempted to discipline your body.

Habit #

32

EXTINGUISH HELL

Hell. Do you think about it much? Not if you're ineffective. Hell is a place that should never creep into your conscious thoughts if you desire to stay in the doldrums of faith.

If you really believed there was a place of eternal torment where friends and family members were headed if they did not know Christ, you would act much differently. You would take every opportunity to tell them about the forgiveness of God. You would pray and petition God for their souls. Nearly every waking moment would bring you before his throne to plead for them.

However, for ineffective Christians hell is a myth. It's meant to scare people, but it's not an actual place. Cultivate the vision of hell as pitchforks and horned devils. Make jokes about it. Laugh when others say, "That's where all the fun people are going." Do not become saddened over such statements.

Above all, you must not read what the Bible has to say about hell, particularly what Jesus said. A correct view of eternal separation from God, where the worm does not die, where there is weeping and gnashing of teeth, would cause you to shudder, cast yourself on the mercy of Almighty God and take your faith more seriously. If such thoughts do come into your mind, immediately think of something happy and tell yourself that God loves everyone and could never be so judgmental as to punish sinful people.

Scripture to Modify: Find words such as *perish, hell* and *torment* in your Bible and place a smiley face over them.

Habit # 33

CHRISTIANITY IS RELIGION, NOT RELATIONSHIP

The way you view your faith has a lot to do with the way you live; therefore you must never think of Christianity as a relationship with God, but as a religion.

A religion is a set of rules, a fixed system of tenets that make people think they are pleasing God. Some religions have stringent rules, while others are more relaxed. You may have to pray three times a day or fast at strategic points on the calendar. Or you might just have to pray before you eat every now and then. Thankfully, the Christian religion can be manipulated so that you don't have to do much at all, just say you believe.

Of course, if you treat your faith as a religion there will be times when you desire to act. There will no doubt be rules you decide to follow that simply make you feel "religious" and not at all like someone who doesn't go to church Sunday mornings.

Whatever your particular bent, never view your faith as a relationship. If you begin thinking about a personal God calling you to holiness and righteous living rather than a set of rules, you have taken a desperately wrong step.

Viewing God as wanting a relationship with you is an unfathomable thought in itself and will cause you to gaze at his glory in a new way. You will begin to want to please him rather than yourself. You will want to know his will instead of your own. Do not get caught in this vicious trap, or you will destroy all the ineffectiveness you have not worked so hard to attain.

Introspection Corner: Do you think God wants a relationship with you? Come on, really? Who do you think you are, anyway?

Habit #

34

APPROACH GOD ONLY TO GET "FIXED"

There are many ways to view God. Ineffective Christians approach him for one reason only: to get a holy "fix."

When you first come to him, you come not out of a sense of your sin and the overwhelming need of forgiveness, nor out of a response to the holiness of God, but because people around you look happy and you want what they have. You come because your wife is about to leave or the doctor has bad news or you're deep in consumer debt. You come to get fixed. To be healed. For a makeover.

Of course effective Christians realize there is a great healing that comes from a relationship with God, but they view it not as a quick fix but as a healing of the soul. They see forgiveness of sin as an eternal issue that supersedes all the temporal needs of earth. Effective Christians serve God in spite of difficulty. You, however, must serve God as long as he meets your needs.

In a church setting this can provide wonderful opportunities to spread the mediocrity. In your evangelism, you can bring in droves of people by simply making the gospel a pill you take to get your needs met. In this view, saying yes to Jesus does not make him Lord, but the great server, the almighty dispenser of health and wealth and perfect smiles.

God is there for you, pal. Teach others this truth and you will sink to new depths of ineffectiveness.

For Further Thought: What need can God meet for you today? If God didn't meet your perceived needs, would you still want to be a Christian? How quickly would you like to be fixed?

Habit # 35

LIVE SUPERSTITIOUSLY

I cannot tell you how many Christians I meet who have found new and creative ways to be ineffective. One I have observed recently is the superstitious Christian.

A superstitious believer is one who puts stock in circumstance and chance. This person believes every occurrence is a sign from the Almighty for whatever decision they're about to make.

If they're looking for a new boyfriend and meet some handsome man whose name is Bill on a train ride into the city, they believe it must be from God because their father's name was Bill, their boss is named Bill, and they got a bill from the electric company that very morning. The fact that the Bill on the train is not a Christian does not concern the person; this is incidental. Bill's middle name is Wayne, and your niece says "waining" instead of "raining," so this is further cause to believe he is Mr. Right.

Other superstitious Christians look at Scripture and discover unique meanings and applications for specific verses. When a banker I know was deciding whether to deal underhandedly in a certain transaction, he read Philippians 2:4: "Each of you should look not only to your own interests, but also to the interests of others." He thought God was telling him to go ahead with the deal as long as he gave a percentage of the interest to the church.

Those who treat the Bible like a horoscope (and actually read their horoscope every day) will be all the more ineffective for it.

Superstitious Steps to Ineffectivity:

Step 1. What important decision do you have to make today?

Step 2. What answer do you most want?

Step 3. Answer those questions, then open your Bible and find a passage that will confirm Step 2.

Habit #

36

LIVE IN THE FUTURE

There are two tenses for the ineffective Christian to reside in. One is the future.

I do not mean by this that the person should consider eternity and life in the hereafter. If a person were to do that, he or she would surely become more effective. I am talking about the future as in tomorrow and next week and next year.

When you were a child you longed to be older. You longed for the responsibility that older children had, then the opportunities teenagers and adults possessed. You did not take advantage of the current moment but lived looking forward to a time that never came. You were never content in the present. This is how you must live out your faith.

If you are in college, you must yearn for the time when you will be out. If you are single, you must yearn to be married. If you are in the midst of your work years, you must long for retirement. If you have small children, you should yearn for an empty nest.

By living in the future you do not take advantage of the present. You do not fully learn in college. You do not take advantage of your singleness or work for God's glory. You do not enjoy the kids' giggles and smiles while they are still around.

This future living could be called an "if only" life. If only I were done with this, I would be happy. Remember, live in the future and you will never truly live in the present.

Question to Ponder: What are you waiting for that's putting your life on hold? Hang on to it today much more tightly.

Habit #

37

LIVE IN THE PAST

If an ineffective Christian is not living in the future, he or she should live in the past. This may be the best way to stay in a state of spiritual decline.

You must understand that many effective Christians use the past for great good. They remember the sin of the past and ask forgiveness. They remember the lessons of the past and act on them. They seek change in themselves because of the past.

I do not want you to do such things. You should longingly desire the past. You must convince yourself it was always better "back then." The hymns were richer. The revivals lasted longer. The fellowship was sweeter. The potluck dinners were not low-fat. The people were more considerate. The missionaries stayed away longer. You didn't have to give as much in the offering to feel good about it.

Unlike the future, which eventually arrives and becomes the present, the past can never come again, so you must bring it back with your mind. Wallow in it. Suck the marrow from the past in your mind, and your eyes will be so glazed that you will not be able to perceive the gift God gives you in the present.

You must always look either backward or forward. Never stand in this moment, the now, and ask what God would have you do for his glory. Do not be content with the smile of a spouse, the purple-orange of the sunset or the feel of a child's hand slipping effortlessly into your own. The smiles, sunsets and hands were always better in the past.

Wise Saying: Constantly compare the past with the present and you will escape any responsibility to change the future.

Habit #

DO NOT VIEW YOUR BODY AS GOD'S TEMPLE

Of all the ways to be ineffective in your Christian life, this habit may be the easiest to master. You must view your body as your own and not God's temple. You may achieve this in a variety of ways.

First, excessive food intake. One of the hallmarks for sub-par Christians is to always want more. This works wonderfully in the area of diet, since you have a daily need of sustenance. God has created in you a natural hunger. The ineffective Christian will take this need and turn it into gluttony. A steak here, a piece of pie there, a Little Debbie Oatmeal Cream Pie (or Star Crunch) on the side, and pretty soon you resemble the *Hindenburg*.

You can also mar God's plan for food by taking too little. Spurning God's little pleasures of fruits and delicacies not only will make you thin but will cause you to feel you are much more spiritual than others. Food intake can lead to gluttony or pride, which are both conduits to ineffectivity.

Since you think about spiritual things at select times, resist the urge to view your body as the lodging place for the Holy Spirit. If for one minute you truly believed that God was making his dwelling inside you, what you eat, what you watch on television, how much time you spend reading the Bible and how you treat your neighbor would all change. Don't view your body as the temple of God; see it as your home, your castle, your private pleasure palace. Eat, drink and be merry! Or starve yourself. It's your party.

Scripture to Avoid: 1 Corinthians 6:19-20

Habit #
39

CULTIVATE PREJUDICE

As a famous ineffective Christian once said—I think it was me—"Judge people by the color of their skin, the language they speak, the clothes they can afford and the way they look, not on the content of their character."

Every day you must cultivate prejudice in your life if you are to live down to my standards. You must set yourself above others in any way possible to show you are superior. Cultivate prejudice by looking down on anyone who is different from you. Skin color, weight, ethnic background, mixed race, height, shoe size or eye color—any of these standards will do.

Caricature people from different parts of the country. Think of snappy things to say about those lazy people from the South, those stupid people from the North, those snobby people from the East or those crazy people out West.

Categorize others. In your mind make certain categories of behavior for people you think are different. This way you will not have to deal with individuals but can, at a glance, judge the motives and intent of anyone on the planet.

Above all, you must not get to know anyone who is different from you, for this would break down stereotypes and cause you to treat others as equals, with respect and with dignity.

Questions to Ponder: Do you have a good friend who is Caucasian? Do you have a good friend who is African-American? Do you have a good friend who is Hispanic? Do you have a good friend who is Native American? If you answered yes to more than one of the above, it is time for you to move.

SHUN JOY

Habit # 40

Every day you choose a way to look at life. Nothing robs you of your ineffectiveness like joy. You must shun it.

Shun joy in the morning when you wake up and notice you have another chance at life. Shun joy when you see the sun rise in splendor. Do not let this sight make you think of the pure light of heaven that is Christ.

Shun joy with your children, particularly when they are small. Notice the diapers, the cuts and scrapes, the whining, crying milieu. Do not for a moment thank God for loaning you these little lives to mold and shape. Do not pick up your child and hold her in your arms for the express purpose of enjoying her. Pick a child up only when you are about to discipline her.

Shun joy as you go about your work. Do not revel in the gifts and talents given you or thank God you can use them to help others.

Shun joy in music. If a particular style makes you light-hearted and desirous of skipping or dancing about the kitchen, tell yourself this is sinful and should not be done by sober-minded people.

Stop smiling, for this is an expression of joy. Squelch any feeling deep within that wants to spring forth in thanksgiving and praise. When you have accomplished the above in your own life, you must spread the feeling to others, which will happen naturally if you follow these directives.

Action Point: Eat a dill pickle and a freshly cut lemon. Immediately look in the mirror. This is how you should appear at all times.

Habit #

41

DON'T BELIEVE JESUS IS THE ONLY WAY TO GOD

Since there are many sincere people in the world who want to be good and work their way to God, you must *not* believe that Jesus is the only way to heaven.

Like the doctrine of hell, belief in the exclusivity of salvation through Jesus is a great motivator for Christians. It compels them to share their faith and spread the word of Christ's claim to lordship.

But you must look at this concept rationally and convince yourself that you are being loving and wise to believe that Jesus isn't the only way. After all, what kind of God would force people to believe something they haven't heard or don't like? That would be cruel, wouldn't it?

Therefore you should foster the belief that all you need is sincerity in your faith. The object of that faith does not matter. It could be Buddha, Muhammad, a stone or a dead ancestor. This chips away at the possibility of absolute truth and the fact that God has the right to make the rules no matter what you think. Further, it puts you in the place of God, which is just where an ineffective Christian should be.

Do not concern yourself with the fields white unto harvest, for if sincerity is the key to faith they don't really need your help. They can find their own way. Just be happy that you have a belief in Jesus and go about your business as usual.

Scripture to Avoid: Acts 4:10-12

Habit #

42

TAKE GRACE FOR GRANTED

One of the great theological truths of Christianity is encompassed in the word *grace*. To have as little effect as possible on those around you, take grace for granted.

You do this by pointing to an aisle you walked long ago as the reference point for your faith. When you are asked, "How do you know you are a Christian?" you should answer, "Because when I was five, I gave up my life of wanton sin and went forward."

Do not consider the fact that God's working in your life today is as much an evidence of his grace as the time you toddled down the aisle in your knickers. If perhaps you do not sense God working, if you do not see a change in behavior and in attitude today, the walk you took as a child may not have meant much and this may be the reason for your ineffectiveness. But you must not think about this; rather continue in this state.

Take grace for granted by sinning and sinning and sinning. When you are convicted about a certain action or pattern of behavior, tilt your head, shrug your shoulders and say, "It's been paid for, no big wup." Live as if God's grace covers every sin with no consequences, and live your ungodliness overtly.

Take grace for granted by condemning others. Never let the words "There but for the grace of God go I" enter your consciousness. A condemning spirit tramples God's grace like an unwanted bug.

Thought for the Day: When you see some unfortunate person, repeat to yourself this phrase: *Boy, I sure am glad I'm better than they are!*

Habit #
43

BELIEVE SEX IS DIRTY

Another way to cultivate ineffective Christian living is to take what God has given as a gift and pervert it or treat it wrongly. This can be achieved with anchovies (on pizza), with blue cheese dressing (on a salad) and especially with sex.

It would be easy for me to encourage you toward sexual promiscuity and debauchery. However, I suggest you treat sex as something inherently nasty, vile, filthy, animal-like and disgusting. This will frustrate your mate to no end and communicate that intimacy is not carried out with the whole person, just the mind. It will also start you on the slippery slope of twisting God's goodness into something unseemly.

If you look at sex between husband and wife as a grotesque, writhing maelstrom, you will miss the opportunity of creatively expressing love to your mate in a physical manner. And if you can take away this expression, pretty soon you can justify the end of any tangible demonstration of love and intimacy.

Confirm your opinion by pointing to all the problems sex wrought in Old Testament days. Then show the negative ways our culture misuses sex to sell products and entice people toward lust, lasciviousness and network miniseries. If this argument held water, of course, you wouldn't be able to breathe.

Remember, the father of lies has twisted all good things provided by the Father of Lights. Believe sex is dirty and treat this gift as a curse.

Scripture to Avoid: The Song of Solomon

Habit #
44

BELIEVE YOU MUST TIDY UP BEFORE COMING TO GOD

The way God views humans is, of course, drastically opposed to the way you should view them if you are to be ineffective. But it is also important to view God in certain ineffective ways. Primarily you need to believe that to approach him, you must be cleaned up. Tidy. Presentable. In order for people to have a relationship with this eternal being, they must get their life in order and *then* pray to him/join a church/sing in the choir.

This mindset will accomplish two things. First, for those who have a particularly sensitive conscience, it will keep them from ever coming to God. They view themselves as utterly sinful the moment they eat the last Chiclet in the box. If they believe they must be tidy in order to have a relationship with God, they will never enter into it, because deep down they know their hearts are wicked.

Second, this mindset causes a false sense of pride in your own holiness. You come to God not recognizing your sin, but feeling that you have pulled yourself up by your spiritual bootstraps and now deserve the favor of the Almighty.

Feeling you must be tidy to come to God will keep you at a distance from him, which is your goal.

When you get the urge to get more involved in church activities, think about how much better everyone else is and wait until you can "get it together." This will not only keep you from growing but also rob your fellow Christians of a nice voice in the choir, helping hands at the homeless shelter or an usher with a firm handshake instead of a dead fish.

For Further Thought: How much work would you have to do to become "tidy" before God today?

Habit #
45

DON'T BE REAL WITH GOD

In my surveys of mediocre Christians, I have noticed a common trait. Nearly 100 percent of them avoid any sense of reality with God. I urge you to duplicate their actions.

Make sure the few moments you devote to prayer during the week do not include expressions from the depths of your being. Do not bring God your disappointments or struggles. Do not tell him how frustrated you are about your gene pool, your high mortgage or the fact that the tip of your cane keeps falling off. Make things nice and pleasant. Deny, deny, deny, particularly if your frustration is really with God.

This again keeps God at a distance from your life and does not acknowledge your true feelings. If you were to hash those things out with your heavenly Father, chances are you would have a quite different view of them when you completed your prayer.

Keeping your deep thoughts and emotions from God also makes you believe that he doesn't already know what is in the depth of your soul. It reinforces the false perception that you can hide things from God. You begin to believe hiding things from him is actually a virtue for those who want to be "spiritual."

Remember the old saying "Never let them see you sweat"? Apply this to God. Never let him see you be real. Practice the same type of dual living you exhibit before your family and friends, thinking and feeling one thing but acting in a totally different way. As you look in the rear-view mirror of life, you'll see your faith become smaller than it actually appears.

Scriptures to Avoid: The Psalms

Habit #

BELIEVE GOD'S WILL IS ELUSIVE & OPPRESSIVE

As I have said, the way you view God is quite important for how much you grow in your Christian life. Therefore, to stay as stagnant as possible, you must see God's will as both elusive and oppressive.

Always pine for direct knowledge from God about any choices you may face. When you do not hear an audible voice from the clouds, this means God is stingy and enjoys playing a celestial game of hide-and-seek with his will. Never mind that he has given you a brain, his Word and the Holy Spirit. You must constantly focus on the fact that he has not stepped out of heaven to tell you whether or not to buy or build a new house.

On the other hand, you should always believe God's will is oppressive in nature. If he did step out of the clouds and give you direct instructions for the details of your life, you must believe he would only give you things that do not satisfy. He will send you to Africa. He will make you single the rest of your life. He will kink your Slinky. Looking at the short-term effects, the temporal rather than the eternal, will help you believe that his will is inherently bad.

Of course, it just may be that God's will for you is where you are right now. He just might be trying to teach you through your present situation. Therefore it is imperative to keep looking elsewhere, believing God is both stingy and mean in his dealings with you.

Scripture to Avoid: Psalm 37:4-5

Habit #

AVOID UNITY IN THE BODY

Ineffective Christians stay to themselves. They do not congregate with others who have the slightest difference in theology or practice. If you truly desire a terminal spiritual life, you will avoid unity at all costs.

If you do not raise your hands in worship, shun those who do. If you dunk, stay away from the sprinklers. If there is a disaster in the community or a worthy cause that could unite people across denominational lines, do not join hands in Christian love, for this would only make the world look on in wonder.

If you should be challenged to associate with someone of another church background, resist the temptation by caricaturing others' beliefs: "You know what those Baptists believe," or "Those Presbyterians think they're better than anybody else," or "Methodists don't like banjos." Concentrate on dogma, not people.

Do not for a moment believe any song that encourages unity. Ineffective Christians believe that in Christ there is East, West, North, South and Middle. They sing, "And they'll know we are Christians by how far apart we are."

If you find disunity unappealing, promulgate the other extreme of false unity. Accept anyone who says they are Christian no matter what they believe about the person of Christ. Warmly welcome those who think Jesus was "simply a good teacher" or "just another of the great prophets." These people may not have their theology down, but they're sincere and really nice.

Remember, you have two options: (1) never accept any shade of theological difference within your fellowship, or (2) water down your congregation with spurious believers. Either extreme will keep you ineffective in your Christian life.

Scriptures to Avoid: Ephesians 4:3; John 17:21

Habit #

LIVE LIKE A CHAMELEON

Authenticity, balance and consistency are marks of the Christian. You should oppose these characteristics with every fiber of your being and live like a chameleon.

A chameleon changes color whenever its surroundings change, and you must as well. When it is Sunday and you are in church, you should smile and present the appearance that you are a spiritual person. But when you reach the water cooler Monday morning, laugh at the off-color jokes and throw in a few barbs at minorities for good measure.

Among racists, you must also be racist. Among gossips, gossip. Among sports fanatics, throw out statistics and memorable plays with the best of them. Among drinkers, drink. Among teetotalers, abstain. In other words, when with pagans, act like a pagan, when with Christians, act like a Christian.

If you begin feeling a slight bit of guilt for your actions, convince yourself that you're living up to the biblical ideal of being all things to all people, when in actuality you're being nothing to anyone but a big fake.

The ineffective Christian believes the most important aspect of life is appearance, so change the way you look and act when you are around people with different values, different priorities and beliefs. The more your life reflects the actions of a chameleon, the more ineffective you will become.

Action Point: Record a phone conversation with a friend from church and a friend from the bowling league. What words were different? How many references to God were made in both?

BE IMPATIENT

Impatience is the second cousin to worry, which is another trait of faithless living. You must pick and prune impatience from day to day and learn how to make every aspect of your life controlled by your own desires.

Be impatient with things. Honk in traffic and run your hands through your hair at every red light. When you are assembling Christmas toys, fixing household appliances, making dinner or waiting for the mail to come, be impatient. Huff about the house because things won't cooperate with your agenda.

Be impatient with people. When someone does not live up to the standards you set, demand that they change. At the grocery store, tap your foot and expel air when the cashier does not ring your food up in record time. Make snide comments about the laziness of toll-booth operators. Scold children for not reaching the car and buckling their seat belts when you're ready to pull out. Snap at your auto mechanic for his lack of attention to your timing chain.

Finally, be impatient with God. Nothing can possibly make you more ineffective than setting demands the Almighty must meet. Keep him apprised of *your* timetable and *your* plans. When he doesn't meet those expectations, take hold of the situation and act quickly.

Under no circumstances should you wait for God to act. Waiting proves you truly trust in God and not yourself.

Scripture to Avoid: Isaiah 40:31

Habit #

50

HAVE ALL THE ANSWERS

No matter what kind of life you lead, you will no doubt come in contact with people who are experiencing troubles and trials. And when people question their faith, it is imperative that you have all the answers.

I do not mean that you should understand the biblical view of suffering. I do not mean you should discern the bedrock theological questions of sincere people. That would be dangerous. I mean you should cultivate an attitude that you have figured out life. You know every question and have snappy answers to boot. Communicate to others that there are no mysteries left to plumb, because you have it all down.

Never just sit and mourn with a friend; say something. Never identify with someone who is struggling. Never simply weep and admit you have felt the same feelings. Give verses, even out of context if you have to. Give short pithy sayings like "This too shall pass." If you can quickly silence a question with a sentence, you have done a great thing, particularly if you can make it rhyme.

You must also take on yourself the weight of the person's problems and believe if you don't have the answers he or she will fall away. If you don't fix the person right then and there, he or she will be lost forever. In this you promote the idea that God is not sovereign, *you* are. He does not control the destiny of the soul and the universe, *you* do. This is why you must act as if you have all the answers.

Action Point: Write out all the answers you have and keep them handy. When trouble comes, you'll need them.

Habit #

51

BECOME A WALKING CLICHÉ

The ineffective Christian not only has all the answers but maximizes his or her points by using clichés.

For example, when you meet someone who has just lost a loved one to a natural disaster, glibly state, "All things work together for good!" Smile knowingly as you repeat this phrase over and over. This demonstrates the awesome hold cliché has on truth.

When a parent agonizes over a child who has gone away to college, shake your head and say, "You really need to let go and let God." This intensifies the pain the person already feels and may cause them to stuff their emotions around those who could truly empathize.

"God said it, I believe it, that settles it!" is a great slogan to use around intellectuals. If someone has made a life study in the sciences, it would be good to caricature their data by saying, "He believes my nearest relative is down at the zoo." Never give an honest ear to a finding that seems to conflict with Scripture. This makes you close-minded and narrow, which is exactly the kind of life an ineffective Christian leads.

Don't just say the clichés, wear them boldly on T-shirts and jackets. Send them on your checks, plaster them on your car, illuminate them during the holidays, and always remember the proverb "A word fitly spoken can be turned into a cliché if you really work at it."

Cliché to Memorize: Jesus is the reason for the season.

Habit #

52

WALK BY SIGHT, NOT BY FAITH

Christians who are rooted in the Bible know God desires a life lived by faith, a total surrender of the will and a casting of oneself on God's mercy. However, if you want to be spiritually ineffective you will walk by sight, not by faith.

Walking by sight means you do not act on the truth revealed in the Scriptures; rather you seek a sign or outward rendering of God to follow. (Such as Gideon's fleece in the Old Testament or, in modern times, Dr. Lacking's electric blanket. I would like to add a word of caution about testing God in this way, because we nearly lost the dear fellow.)

Walking by sight will cause you to follow God only when you feel he is leading you. In the night, when you are alone, filled with doubt and fear for the future, you should not reflect on God's faithfulness in the past. You should not cast your eyes on the word and realize how much the Father cares for you. Instead lean on your own understanding. Judge God by what you can see happening around you.

Walk by sight in the big decisions of life. Walk by sight in the small ones. Do not put any of your hope in things that cannot be seen, such as heaven, and you will live a gloriously ineffective Christian life.

Ineffective Reminder: Always unplug your fleece.

Habit #
53

BE A SPIRITUAL WEENIE

The bible and church history are filled with accounts of men and women who stood up for their beliefs and their God. However, the ineffective Christian will learn the plethora of ways he or she can become a spiritual weenie.

Remember, becoming a weenie is a choice. A process. First you must convince yourself that restraint is the better part of valor. If you find yourself in a situation where you think it might be good to speak up or act on a spiritual matter, hold back because you want others to see how truly winsome you are.

If an unbeliever who has no idea of your religiosity takes a few jabs at the church, the Bible and God, do not be prepared with a reasoned answer. You must keep the hope that is within you bottled up for fear that someone might begin attacking you.

Perhaps you will find yourself among church people who begin gossiping and slandering someone in the fold. At this point you must never rebuke them, for it might make their self-esteem plunge. Instead laugh, nod your head and join in the skewering of your fellow believer.

As you progress through various levels of weenieness, you will find it easier to live a limp faith. You will look throughout the centuries at people who have been jailed, mocked, scorned and even killed for their belief in God. You will not want to become a statistic. As much as possible keep your faith to yourself and your head on your shoulders. As someone wise once said, look out for number one.

Scripture to Avoid: 1 Peter 3:15

Habit #

54

BELIEVE SPIRITUAL WARFARE IS FICTION

Everyone knows how much fun Frank Peretti has had with angels and demons warring in the heavenlies. If you are to live ineffectively as a Christian, you must never believe there is such a thing as a spiritual battle.

Angels are meant to be trinkets you hang on Christmas trees. They are ornaments for festive people. They are fads, showing up in secular and sacred books and calendars. Interest in angels should be encouraged as long as the truth about them is never explored. Angels are playthings, not reality.

Conversely, demons should be considered the "dark side" of the playground, the yang to the yin. Demons are needed to balance out the stories told around the spiritual campfire, the villains of our tales of faith.

Under no circumstances should you read the Old Testament, which assumes the reality of angels. Under no circumstances should you read any prophetic literature like Revelation. However, if you do happen onto any of these passages, convince yourself that angels are simply metaphors of God's light and goodness.

If you were to take the spiritual battle seriously and the fight that is going on for the souls of humanity, you would no doubt pray more, seek to live a holier life and strive to tell others the good news. You would see heavenly angels as your ally in this fight and fallen angels as part of the enemy's dastardly plan. You would take on the weapons of warfare and wade into the battle.

Don't do this. Spiritual warfare is fiction.

Scripture to Avoid: Ephesians 6:12

Habit #
55

JUDGE OTHERS

Ineffective Christians have a tendency to look past their own sin. This is very good. One of the best ways to continue in this state is to look at others in a spirit of judgment.

Judge others' actions. When you see the child of a friend do a bit of mischief, judge the parents for their lack of discipline in the home.

Judge others' words. Be so picky about grammar that people are afraid to speak around you. If a subject and a verb disagree, stop others in midsentence to correct them. Judge accents. Judge the choice of words, saying, "You don't mean *vital,* you mean *integral.* There's a difference." This puts you above others and makes you feel superior. However, you should judge unkind words only when they are spoken about you.

Judge others' motives. Cultivate the uncanny ability to get into the minds of others so that you know exactly what they are thinking and why they do certain things. It is imperative that you relate these truths to friends: "The pastor preached that sermon because he struggles with that sin," or, "The elders want a gymnasium built so they can put their names on the front of the building."

Do not show grace to others. Do not give the benefit of the doubt. Never take someone at face value for what they say or do. And when someone says, "Judge not, lest ye be judged," believe their motives are impure as well.

Thought to Ponder: If others judged you the way you judge others, how would your church be different? Would we need altars or gallows?

Habit #

56

OVERANALYZE EVERY SITUATION

Pop psychology has provided a number of wonderful conduits for ineffectivity. Overanalyzing a situation rather than calling it sin is one of the best. I urge you to sit down with a good self-help book and begin today.

It is important that you emphasize self-esteem. "I'm only acting this way because my self-esteem is low." You can use this excuse for everything from an outburst of anger to murder. It may be true that your self-esteem is low, but you must exploit the term for maximum effect.

Overanalyze others, and it will either drive them crazy or wear them down to the point where they eventually agree with your assessment. "You're obese not because of these empty potato-chip bags, but because of the way the mailman used to deliver postcards to you when you were a child."

Overanalyzing may serve you best when there's nothing wrong and no sin has been committed, but because of your keen senses others begin to believe there's something wrong. "The pastor's wife wore that dress because she secretly resents the congregation," or, "You don't like my chicken casserole because your inner child abhors poultry." When someone at church doesn't greet you in just the right way, judge them. Believe the worst, that they suddenly hate you and want to do terrible things to your pets while you're away on vacation.

The key is always looking at the psychological, not the spiritual, component of people's actions. Remember, you will be most ineffective when you overanalyze others.

Action Point: Overanalyze why you are reading this book. What is the deep, dark secret that caused you to choose it? You want to buy another, don't you?

Habit #
57

SCARE OR SKIRT WHEN TALKING ABOUT GOD

Let me pose two conversation scenarios you should set up while sitting beside strangers. Many Christians feel guilty for not sharing the gospel more often in these situations, but as an ineffective believer, you must seize the moment to be as ineffective as possible.

The scene is an airport terminal. You are on a business trip for your company.

PERSON 1: Are you heading to Portland on business?

YOU: Yes.

PERSON 1: It's supposed to be nice there today.

YOU: Good.

PERSON 1: I see you carry a Bible in your briefcase. Why?

YOU: I don't know. Maybe my wife stuck it in there.

PERSON 1: So, are you one of those Christians?

YOU: Look, can't a guy carry a Bible without being interrogated? It's not against the law, you know.

This is "the skirt." Whenever an opportunity arises to speak about God, you must do an end run around the conversation. Make the other person feel guilty for bringing it up.

The other extreme works nicely as well. It is called "the scare."

PERSON 2: Are you heading to Portland on business?

YOU: Yes, the Lord has called me to Portland. He talks to me, you know.

PERSON 2: Really? Well, uh . . . it's supposed to be nice there today.

YOU: Well, praise God! Would you like to pray and become a Christian right now?

PERSON 2: Uh, I think I have to change flights, excuse me.

Action Point: Find someone today at a bus stop, on an airplane or in an elevator and use one of the above.

Habit #

58

LIVE A SAFE LIFE

You have heard it said that the Christian life is a great adventure. You have heard it said that the world has not seen what God can do through a person totally surrendered to him. But you may not have heard that the ineffective life is the safe life.

Do not take chances with your existence. Do not consider going to places where there is persecution and where people have been known to criticize Christians. You certainly should never consider living where Christians are mocked, scorned and even killed. This could seriously hamper your golf game.

You really need to keep yourself safe financially. If you're thinking about Christian service of some kind, do not jump into things. Take a few years. Make a little money. Get a nest egg saved up and then decide if you want to do something foolish.

Keep yourself safe physically by buying a home in the suburbs or in a rural area. Do not live in the inner city where crime and poverty reign. Build walls between your congregation and your community. Do not try to minister to people who have serious diseases. Leave that to little women from Calcutta who don't have the sense to come in out of the slums.

Keep yourself safe spiritually by avoiding any direct contact with the enemy of your soul. If you sense antagonism or some kind of spiritual warfare, withdraw immediately. You may put yourself in danger. Remember, self-preservation is the most important thing for the ineffective believer.

Introspection Corner: In what ways can I shrink from stepping out in faith and make my life less of an adventure?

Habit #

59

EMBRACE THE TRIANGLE OF MEDIOCRITY

There are many ways to look at the ineffective life, and since most ineffective people are visual, I present the Triangle of Mediocrity.

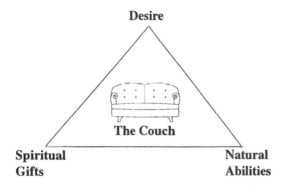

Desire

The Couch

Spiritual Gifts

Natural Abilities

At the bottom right corner of the triangle you see your natural abilities. These are the things you do in your own strength. These are talents and bents you have. Your triangle should lean heavily toward this end.

In the bottom left is "spiritual gifts." If you are ineffective, you probably are oblivious to your spiritual gifts. Do not try to discover them. You can only harm yourself if you acknowledge God's intervention in your life.

167

At the top of the triangle is your desire. This represents what drives your life. In the spiritually minded person, desire fuels gifts and abilities. In you, desire should be focused on self or the middle of the triangle, the couch.

Action Point: Analyze your life in relation to the triangle of mediocrity. In what ways must you change to become more unbalanced?

Habit #

60

PUT YOUR FAITH IN ONE PERSON

Since it is very difficult to follow a God you cannot see or feel or hear, one habit that invariably leads to ineffective Christianity is to place your faith in a person.

This may be a pastor or teacher in your church, but it might be better to choose some well-known author, speaker or celebrity. These are people you only see from a distance. You have no ability for a close relationship with them, so it's easier to put them on a pedestal.

You must idolize this person. Quote the person in daily conversation. Say things like "You know what [IDOL] says about that, don't you?" Buy autographed copies of your idol's books. Place this individual on the same par with the apostles and prophets, and follow even the most inane statements made by the person.

Instead of studying the Bible yourself, follow your idol's particular theological bent. Do not dig into particularly difficult passages; turn to your "authority." In this way you put the person in the place of God, and anyone put in God's place will eventually let you down.

When the person you idolize is exposed as a human being in all his or her frailty, you must be shocked senseless. Drown in self-pity and continue your spiritual depression for days. Be tempted to lose your faith, and tell others that God has let you down, when in reality it wasn't God you were trusting in the first place.

Action Point: Write a letter to a famous Christian today and ask for a handkerchief or worn sock to keep with you always.

Habit #

61

SPEAK CHRISTIANESE

As you can tell from this book, hiding your faith "under a bushel" is one great way to remain mediocre. There is another way to douse the light of faith and still verbalize your belief in Christianity. This use of language will marginalize your message and make you incomprehensible to the watching world. Whenever you are afforded the opportunity, speak "Christianese."

Christianese is that rare language of those in the "in" club. If you learn to master its usage, you will feel like you're part of the inner circle of the righteous, whether you are or not. It's easy to mistake the real thing for a counterfeit when listening to Christianese.

A few favorite phrases of the language are

- born again
- a real blessing in my life
- asked Jesus into my heart
- let me share this with you
- what a time of fellowship we had
- Jesus is my *personal* Savior
- the Spirit really spoke to me

These phrases are harmless in themselves, but when used liberally they become a cacophony of spiritual goo. Do not seek to communicate truth to your audience, do not seek to understand the message yourself, seek only to know the holy lingo and spread it around.

Being able to speak this language will eventually cause you to take for granted the things you are saying. You will become so proficient in speaking Christianese that it will simply roll off the tongue like an aimless salvo at the firing range.

Action Point: Write your testimony using Christianese so your message will be incomprehensible to anyone but you. It will really be a blessing to your heart.

Habit #

62

PRACTICE SPIRITUAL PROCRASTINATION

I put off writing this chapter for quite some time. In the grand scheme of ineffective living, this discipline is better than failing to finish a task.

Spiritual procrastination is the process by which you convince yourself you are aiming high while actually achieving nothing. Spiritual procrastination seems on the surface to vault you to a deeper level of faith, but in reality it keeps you mired in the sludge of mediocrity.

For example, let's say you desire to read through the Bible in one year. It's a commendable goal and makes you look good. Since January is the month for beginnings, search diligently for just the right translation with just the right study notes. Consult friends, pastors and bookstore owners. In two or three months you will have no excuse not to go out and buy it, but you must shop around for the best price. Like its secular counterpart, spiritual procrastination will not allow you to act on anything unless you've taken enough time to feel really guilty about it.

When you hear yourself saying, "You know, I really need to just get moving on buying this Bible," it will be summer. And since you simply can't start something as big as reading through the entire Bible during any month but January, you take at least six months to get prepared and spread the word around.

The motto of a spiritual procrastinator is always "Why not put off till tomorrow what you could easily do today?" Follow this and you will reach new lows of Christian complacency.

Question to Ponder: What spiritual effort can I put off today that will enhance my ineffectivity?

Habit #
63

BELIEVE NEW IS ALWAYS BETTER

There is a great treasure available to you in the history of the church. Therefore I urge you, ineffective ones, that you reject anything that's been around more than ten years.

Stay away from great hymns. Never study the words to "Amazing Grace," for you may see how much a wretch you really are. Never sing "Holy, Holy, Holy," for you may catch a glimpse of the purity and splendor of the Almighty.

Because those around you may not know what a "royal diadem" is, shun "All Hail the Power of Jesus' Name." Some may be offended that God is described as having "chariots of wrath," so stay away from "O Worship the King." Others will no doubt protest the military nature of "A Mighty Fortress," so do not let this hymn be included in your repertoire.

Do not stop at music, however. You must shun things such as the Apostles' Creed. Denigrate the sermons of Spurgeon, the writings of Chambers and books without a market niche. By doing so, you separate yourself from those who have written and voiced their faith throughout the ages. You make their contribution to the faith and succeeding generations patently nil, and raise the standard of contemporaneity as the most important.

If you cannot plow these songs and texts under the soil of church history, change their words to make them seem new, which is something like changing the nose on the *Mona Lisa*.

Action Point: Rewrite the text to "I Know Whom I Have Believed," changing the title to "Hey, I'm Happy Today!"

Habit #

64

RUSH TO EASTER & SKIP GOOD FRIDAY

Good Friday is one of those holidays you should just let slip by without much fanfare. Of course you should let your children get into the eggs and the bunnies and pretty outfits that cloud Easter fairly well, but I find that those who are ineffective treat Good Friday with a blasé attitude.

Good Friday isn't as easy to celebrate as Easter or Christmas. You don't say, "Merry Good Friday!" to people passing. You don't have a warm, fuzzy crèche and a baby to catch your attention. You have spikes driven in flesh, a crown of thorns on a pure head, and a crude, splinter-laden cross.

Good Friday reminds you of the suffering Christ endured for your sin. Good Friday shows you the extent to which God would go to redeem your soul. One thought of the punishment of Jesus on the cross, and half the things you do during the day would be reevaluated.

Therefore, you must not think about it much. Rush to Easter. Do not dwell on the crucifixion. Do not linger on the passion of Christ, his blood spilled for you, his hands and side pierced. Run to the empty tomb first. Dodge the scenes of agony. Skirting Good Friday makes your holiday much more positive. People will feel less sensitive over the price God paid to obtain their salvation.

Ineffective Exercise: To better celebrate the meaning of the day, use Good Friday to get things done around the house.

Habit #

65

MARGINALIZE CHRISTMAS

This one seems so obvious, but it remains one of the best ways to keep Christians from focusing on the truth of Christianity. In your preparation for the holiday, you must marginalize the real message of Christmas.

First, marginalize Christmas to your non-Christian friends. This can be as simple as saying the cliché you learned in Habit #51, "Jesus is the reason for the season!" Say it again and again. Or go to the other extreme and say nothing about the real meaning behind the holiday. Let your Christian ornaments do the talking. Whichever method you find most ineffective, choose and use it.

Marginalize Christmas to society. Make them think that your one mission in life is to get the crèche on the courthouse lawn, rather than to communicate the truth of Christ. Bring lawsuits, congregate angry mobs, and demand your right to free speech rather than speaking winsomely about the Savior.

Marginalize Christmas in your life. It is so important that you make *things* paramount in your celebration. Desire the right tree, the perfect gift, the largest turkey, the right amount of snow and so on. Fret about the length of the tinsel. Make Christmas a living hell for those around you because you want it to be just right.

Whatever you do, never let it enter your mind that Christmas is for anyone else but you. Do not seek to give, but to receive.

Action Point: Write a sentence that tells the true meaning of Christmas. Remember to put in all the things you want this year.

Habit #
66

FILL YOUR LIFE WITH NOISE

Pascal said, "Uh . . ." Well, I'm really not sure what the quote is and I'm too lazy to look it up, but the gist of it was that inside each of us is a vacuum, not the Eureka or Bissell kind but a hole that must be filled by something. Ineffective believers seek to fill that hole with noise.

Noise comes from many sources, but chiefly the media. Fill your days with endless chatter and information from the radio, television, videos, games and CD-ROM. As you travel from room to room you should always seek to have something *on.* Wake to a clock radio and keep one in the shower as well (battery-powered only—we want you ineffective, not deceased).

When you enter your car, flip on the radio or plug in a tape. Pretty soon you will become accustomed to having this background always with you, and you will feel uncomfortable without it. Invest in a good headset that stays with you at all times.

Keep the noise going at parties, before church begins and especially when you are in the same room with your children. If there is no noise to buoy your relationships, you are more likely to begin deep conversations and get to know each other on a new level. The noise keeps people at a distance and, best of all, keeps you from thinking about God.

Action Point: What noise do you hear right now as you are reading this book? Do you hear the radio? the air conditioner? television? If not, quickly turn something on before you have a deep thought.

Habit #

67

BE A POOR RECEIVER

There is nothing more exasperating for people in the church than a person who will not take anything, will not receive from others and will only give. If you are such a person I applaud you, for it means that in your zeal you are being ineffective.

When someone kindly offers to watch your children and give you a break for a few hours, do not accept. Laugh and tell them how much you love your kids and how you can't stand spending time without them. If the person persists, let your children go for forty-five minutes then keep your friend's children for two weeks in the dead of winter.

If you have a specific need, like hospitalization, do not let anyone cook meals for you. Insist that you can make it on your own and shun the goodness of others. In fact, you might pick up a few gifts to distribute on your way home from intensive care.

Over time, if you learn the art of not accepting anything from others, you will subtly convey the notion that you are not weak like common folk. You have pulled yourself up by your bootstraps and will continue to do so. Feel proud when people say, "I don't think she'd even let someone bury her."

You may believe you do not deserve to be helped. You may think there are so many people with bigger problems that you don't want to enjoy the fruits of God's grace given by others. Whatever the reason, by not accepting gifts you thwart the joy your friends get in giving and hoard it all to yourself.

Habit Thought: A gift spurned each day keeps grace away.

Habit #
68

MAKE YOUR SPOUSE MEET ALL YOUR NEEDS

As with coming to God, an ineffective Christian marries for one reason: to get his or her needs met. The following four attitudes will make your marriage all it shouldn't be.

1. The deep need of every person is companionship. You do not want to be lonely for the rest of your life, so you should marry. Make your spouse ease that deep need in your soul.

2. Intimacy takes many forms. Closeness, tenderness and sex are all aspects of it. However, you must believe that such things are for your gratification alone and that the person you are married to exists to make you feel satisfied.

3. Each person needs security. We want to know that financially, physically and emotionally we can depend on someone. However, the ineffective believer clings to his or her spouse like a ball and chain and feels secure only when the other is present.

4. Ultimately you must look to your spouse to meet your spiritual needs. When the other is attuned to God, you are as well. Likewise, when the other is in a religious funk, your relationship with God is in the pits.

In healthy marriages these four areas work to build a relationship, forging an unbreakable bond. But the ineffective marriage looks like host and parasite, one sucking the life from the other. If you rely on your spouse to meet all your needs, you will make both of your lives miserable in the end. After all, you have put a mere mortal in the place where only God belongs.

Action Point: In what ways have you made your spouse meet your needs? What new ways can you find to exploit him or her today?

Habit #

69

MAKE WORSHIP OPTIONAL

I have already touched on several issues of the spiritual life, like prayer and fasting, Bible reading and evangelism, but one of the best secrets for ineffective living is the habit of making worship optional.

I am not talking about sporadic church attendance, though that does help. I am speaking about your attitude, your outlook, the very core of your being. I am speaking about what goes through your mind when you read a passage of Scripture or see a natural wonder in creation. I am dealing with your reaction to topics like God's love, his grace, forgiveness and holiness.

For committed Christians it is impossible to look at Scripture or a sunrise and not worship God from the depth of the soul. It is impossible to ponder God's holiness without a sense of wonder and awe. But I encourage you to think of worship as something you do only when you are singing in a formal service. Worship should not be a minute-by-minute lauding of a loving God, but a few sentences of responsive reading you do every third week.

Think of worship as a nebulous add-on, a holy option. You read your Bible, study a few verses, sing a few songs, and at some point in all of those activities you worship, though you're really not sure where. Convince yourself that worship can't be planned, it just has to happen. In this way worship becomes an event rather than a lifestyle.

Questions to Ponder: When was the last time you felt you really worshiped God? How can you avoid such an experience in the future?

Habit #

70

KEEP A RELIGIOUS SCORECARD

Vital to the ineffective believer is a plumb line, a measuring stick for spirituality, for if you are to truly embrace mediocrity you must be able to keep a religious scorecard.

Keeping such a record, which is a euphemism for living by the law, not only will make you feel better about the way you live but will keep you above others you seek to compete with.

For example, if you go to a church that has Sunday-morning, Sunday-evening and Wednesday-night services, you score higher on the spiritual Richter scale than those whose church has only a Sunday-morning service and small groups. Even if you don't attend all the services at your church, you rank higher because you look better.

Give yourself points for having the right translation of the Bible. Wear conservative colors and culottes and judge those who are seen in jeans. Length of hair, absence of makeup, and a car with religious slogans all add to your total.

Whatever is outward, whatever looks good, whatever seems spiritual on the surface, seek after these things and you will be living by the law. It is imperative that you not lean on scriptural principles for your spiritual criterion, but look to your own inner sense of what is right. This will keep you and those around you basking in ineffective living for years to come.

Thought for the Day: A religious scorecard is kept for only one reason: to win.

PUT GOD IN A BOX

Your concept of God has a great deal to do with the way you live your life. This is why you must limit God or put him in a box.

Two extremes are prevalent in the church today, so I suggest you gravitate toward one of them. The first way to put God in a box is to demand that he obey you. If someone you know has an illness, command God to heal her. If you are short on cash, pray earnestly for money to drop into your lap. In this extreme God is simply the heavenly valet you order from task to task.

By using this method you imply the belief that God revolves around you and is there to glorify you. Angels are at your beck and call; visions, tongues and all manner of miracles are yours.

Another excellent way to put God in a box is to deny the Almighty the ability to work in people's lives. Anything that smells of the miraculous must be discarded because "I don't think God works that way anymore." If someone experiences a life-changing event you've never had, explain that they are mistaken and repeat the phrase "He only did that in the first century."

As much as you are able, make God conform to your image and what you believe he ought to be like. Do not leave room for him to act in any way he pleases. Believe he must first ask your permission.

Thoughts to Ponder: What boxes have you put God in lately? What would happen if you didn't put him in a box?

Habit #
72

HOLD GRUDGES

Like the elephant, the ineffective Christian finds it hard to forget things, particularly the unpleasant ones. If you are to remain lukewarm in your faith, you must learn the fine art of holding grudges.

Of course a good grudge is one that is aged in anger, festering in the soul over many years. This could be a grudge you had against a classmate, teacher or bus driver from childhood.

But I find the best grudges, the ones that really debilitate your faith, are ones held against others in the church family. These could be instances where you were intentionally or unintentionally treated badly.

First tell yourself you have the right to be angry. This is the "mull" stage. Then move from the mull to active hatred. Begin thinking of terrible things you'd like to do to that person or their family members. The third stage is "holding." A grudge does you no harm unless you continually pull it out, poke it, prod it or mentally play with it.

Under no circumstances should you forgive the other person. You should never think, *God has forgiven me so much, I should not hold this against them any longer.* Stay away from the concept of grace and make them pay for what they did! The more grudges you can hold at the same time, the more ineffective you'll become.

Action Point: Think of someone who did you wrong many years ago. Now grit your teeth. Imagine them being embarrassed in a social situation. Smile. Repeat the process.

Habit #
73

APPROACH CHURCH LIKE A CONSUMER

Committed Christians know the value of a good church. They desire worship, see needs, plug in, help out, get involved. However, ineffective Christians do not look for ways to serve, but for ways to change things for their own good.

You must approach church like a consumer. Hop from one congregation to the next, keeping a careful list of positives and negatives such as: Church A's pastor preaches only fifteen minutes, but the refreshments at Church B are always fresher. Church C has a splendid sound system that never squeals, while Church D has a paved parking lot.

Do not judge a church by how much people love each other and are committed to discipleship. Do not judge a church by the ability of the pastor to teach God's Word. You must judge a church by your own selective criteria and choose a place of worship as you would a loaf of bread or a dishwashing detergent. You must judge a church by how it makes you feel when you walk out the door on Sunday morning.

A good approach is to not decide on a place of worship. Keep the pastor and the congregation in a state of limbo about your involvement. Say things like "We're not sure we want to go here because we don't think the youth group would be right if we started having kids."

If you have been living in an area for more than a year and still haven't found a church, good job!

Thought to Ponder: Remember, the church exists for one reason, to please you.

NEVER DRINK FROM LIVING WATER

Habit #74

If you follow the habits listed so far in this book, you will probably not have a problem with Habit #74. But perhaps you will come to a point in your spiritual life where you desire more than anything to know God. Remote as the possibility may seem, there may be a time when your heart will cry out to God and you will thirst for him with an unquenchable passion and desire him above all else.

If this ever happens to you, and you still want to remain ineffective, remember to drink from temporal waters and not the living water. In order to do this you must follow the single biggest "Do Not" of the ineffective Christian.

DO NOT READ THE BIBLE.

Follow your inner voice. Read books that offer easy steps to fulfillment. You can even read what others say about the Bible, but under no circumstances are you to read the Bible.

You must seek to drink from temporal waters, leaning on counselors, friends, your job, television or a time-management guru. Lean on anything that will take the ache in your soul away from you, but do not read the Bible.

Reading the Bible is dangerous because a transformation takes place when you put yourself under the spotlight of God's Word. You see your sin. You see your need for God. You will yearn for him and him alone. If you begin reading the Bible for yourself, pretty soon nothing will satisfy you until you know God intimately.

Scripture to Avoid: John 7:37-38

Habit #

75

GUIDE OTHERS WITH GUILT

Guilt is a rather sensitive topic. But lukewarm Christians must realize that guilt can help maximize their ineffectiveness and spread it to others.

Think of guilt as cholesterol. Some of it is good for your diet; much of it is bad. In the same way good guilt causes you to cast yourself on the mercy of God. It pushes you toward repentance and forgiveness. Bad guilt is something you use on other people to motivate and manipulate. You, of course, should use bad guilt.

For example, if you are given the task of recruiting Sunday-school teachers, you must not pray earnestly and ask God to take control of the situation; you must grab guilt by the horns and wrack people's lives with it. Say things like "I'd like you to consider teaching our third-graders this year—that is, unless you don't think children are important," or, "I saw you going to a ballgame the other night. It's a shame you couldn't spend half that time to prepare a lesson for the kids in our sixth-grade class."

If others do not respond to your call on their lives, make them feel guilty. Bring up their past wrongs, shame them and urge them to do what you want in order to make God like them again. If they still refuse, knit your brow, fold your arms and sternly say, "I'll be praying that God will change your heart."

Guilt is the best motivator for the ineffective Christian. Use it today to your best advantage.

Bumper Sticker: Have you made a friend feel guilty today?

Habit #

76

LOOK FOR SIGNIFICANCE IN ALL THE WRONG PLACES

Each person on Planet Earth longs to be known, to be heard, to make a difference. We want our lives to be significant. This is a God-given desire. However, you must look for significance in all the wrong places.

First, look for it in people. The more well-known people you can say you know, the more significant you will be. The number of autographed copies of successful books and phone numbers of important people you possess correlates to a life of significance.

But don't stop there. Look for significance in things. Get your feeling of worth from the amount of money you make, the number of rungs you've progressed in your company, how close your personal parking space is to the front door. Cars, clothes, houses, books published and even plush carpeting are all valid "significance builders."

To be honest, it doesn't really matter where you look for significance as long as you do not look for it in your relationship with God. It is valid, of course, to work for God's favor, to compare your spiritual accomplishments to those of others in order to gain significance. But your significance should never be based on the premise that God loves you and you are his child. Never let yourself rest in the fact that you are a son or daughter of the King of Kings and that God could not love you more than he does this very moment.

Action Point: Whose name can you drop today to make others feel you are important?

Habit #

77

DON'T FINISH WHAT YOU START

Growing Christians learn that it is vital to complete tasks they believe God has given them. But the ineffective Christian discovers how good it is to begin many things but finish just a few.

One great place to start is Bible reading. I suggest you promise to read the entire Bible in the next year, then stop somewhere between Adam and Moses.

Small groups are the bane of ineffective Christians since they promote personal growth and accountability. Begin going to such a group, then drop out after two or three meetings because you're "overextended."

Commit yourself to any number of church committees and fail to fulfill your obligation. Teach a Sunday-school class for half a quarter. Write half of an encouraging letter to a missionary, then abandon it because you aren't sure where you put the address.

The most important thin

Editor's note: We are very sorry the author did not get us the complete manuscript in time for publication, but we feel he has illustrated his point by example nicely.

Ineffective Christianity: A Personal Test

This helpful scientific exam will aid you in evaluating your spiritual state of being. Please answer each question as honestly as possible, circling the appropriate letter. Ineffective answers are listed immediately following the test.

1. The Bible is . . .
   a. my guide.
   b. the "Good Book."
   c. on the coffee table under the newspaper. (Or try the car or maybe the magazine rack. It's around, I saw it last week.)
2. People know I'm a Christian because . . .
   a. I love God with all my being and others as myself.
   b. I go to church every Sunday, except when there's a really big game on.
   c. There's a fish symbol on my car.
3. I've talked to someone about Christ . . .
   a. in the last week.
   b. in the last year.
   c. in the last decade, if you count saying "God bless you" to someone who sneezed in the doctor's office.

4. When faced with a moral or ethical dilemma I . . .
   a. try to find Scripture that sheds light on the subject.
   b. pray and seek godly counsel.
   c. toss a coin and cross my fingers.
5. The biggest priorities in life in order are . . .
   a. God, my family, my work.
   b. my family, God, my work.
   c. my work, my family, my stamp collection, my part-time business, my computer, God.
6. I determine how much I will give to my church by . . .
   a. a percentage of my gross income.
   b. a percentage of my _____ income.
   c. how much change I happen to have with me.
7. Communion is meaningful for me because . . .
   a. I celebrate the death, burial and resurrection of Christ.
   b. I reflect on my sins and spend time confessing them before God.
   c. it's always at the end of the service and that means I'm only ten minutes from lunch.
8. Spiritual warfare is . . .
   a. something important I'm aware of.
   b. something going on in the heavenlies.
   c. something Frank Peretti made a lot of money writing about.

9. The ultimate goal for my life is . . .
   a. to hear God say, "Well done, faithful servant."
   b. to lead others to Christ by my words and my example.
   c. to be happy.
10. True joy comes from . . .
   a. a close relationship with God.
   b. a close relationship with other people.
   c. being left alone by God and other people.

Answers

1. c. (True ineffective Christians have no idea where to find their Bible.)
2. b and c. (Fish symbols and other paraphernalia exempt you from saying or doing anything about your faith.)
3. c.
4. c. (Some people think there's a verse for everything, and that's just not true.)
5. c. (Your computer may be higher on the list.)
6. c. (The trick is not making the offering plate jangle with your dimes and nickels.)
7. c. (Isn't it a great feeling to know your weekly obligation is almost over?)
8. c.
9. c. (What else is there?)
10. c. (True ineffectiveness can be achieved only in isolation.)

AWAY WITH THE MANGER

A Spiritually Correct
Christmas Story

To Reagan Michael
on your first Christmas

"Subscriptions went up, tolerance went down, and I don't want to talk about my blood pressure."

BETTY STANTON, PUBLISHER, *HARTVILLE DAILY NEWS*

"These people need to get over their love affair with the manger."

DIERDRA BERGMAN FREEP, PRESIDENT,
ATHEISTS AGAINST MANGERS

"In the Old Testament, God spoke from a bush, in a cloud and even through a donkey. This year he surprised us all and used Jackson Grim."

THE REVEREND MARTY KARLSEN, PASTOR,
HARTVILLE COMMUNITY CHURCH

"What do you want, Mary? . . . You want the moon?"

GEORGE BAILEY, *IT'S A WONDERFUL LIFE*

INTRODUCTION

The truth is, it was just one column. Nothing extraordinary. Every day I write one, hand it to the editor and move on to the next. I never expected what happened, but then who can predict such things?

I still don't know who sent that first letter with the song. It could have been one of those crazy fundamentalists. Judging from what happened to our town, it could have been an angel. I think the whole thing was like a saucepan filled with too much popcorn. It was only a matter of time before the lid blew off, and I just happened to be the one holding on when it did.

I was accused of many things during that Christmas season. The religious right said I was a liberal with an agenda. The local atheist, Dierdra Bergman Freep, branded me a closet conservative trying to impose my values. There were a few who thought I was a congenital liar and had made the whole thing up just to be ornery or to sell papers.

The facts are simple. I found a good letter with a humorous song, and I was staring at a deadline. Period. No agenda. I wasn't fishing for an award. I just had a column to write.

I suspect it's the same feeling a mother gets when the cupboards are bare and her husband and kids show up hungry for dinner. You make the most with what you've got. That's all I did.

So I wrote the column, and believe me, this town hasn't been the same. That year we argued over the establishment clause and debated the lemon test. We had no idea how much words can affect a town. Now we do.

I never thought of myself as anything but a columnist, so I was surprised when they asked me to tell this story in a book. Most folks couldn't find Hartville on a map if you circled it for them, and we're so small I doubt if we would go through half the first printing of this book if each family bought ten copies. But I suppose publishers know more about things like that than I do.

I would like to thank Hartville Radio for their help in recreating transcripts from certain broadcasts, and the creative writers who penned the alternate Christmas song texts.

And I wish to thank the Snuggle Slipper Factory.

> *Jackson Grim*
> *Columnist, Hartville Daily News*

THE LETTER

I was crawling out from under the mail after Thanksgiving, wishing I hadn't taken those two days off. I always gain twenty pounds and do twice the work the next week to catch up. Plus, it takes me at least a month to get the turkey smell off my hands, and then it's time for Christmas, when we do it all over again.

I had twenty letters on the desk that morning, not counting junk mail. Five were from irate Hartville Cablevision customers complaining about my light-hearted column on the recent channel change. I interviewed "The Cable Fairy" in the column. I thought it was pretty creative, but for some reason changing channels on these people throws their life into a tailspin. One day they're watching the Home Shopping Network and the next it's ESPN, and they don't know what to do.

I filed those letters and moved on to the other hate mail from gun owners, religious wackos and fans of a certain talk radio host who shall remain nameless. It was a pretty ordinary stack.

Then I saw a letter addressed to "The Columnist." There was no return address, and it didn't have postage. I figured someone had dropped it in interoffice mail. Could have been anybody inside or outside the paper.

I held it up to the light to check for plastic explosives. You can't be too careful these days. It looked clean, so I opened it.

Here's what I saw:

November 27
To The Columnist
Hartville Daily News

I am responding to your article concerning the City Council's decisions to ban and then marginalize our manger scene. As you may know, the crèche display is a tradition in our town that spans some decades. For more than fifty years Hartville has enjoyed a simple scene with a stable, animals, some shepherds, Mary, Joseph and the baby Jesus on the lawn in front of the city building. For some reason this scene has become offensive to a few. Though it is a replication of an historical occurrence supported by eyewitness accounts, it is not politically correct. This decision is supposedly for the good of all Hartville.

In a conciliatory effort by the council, in accordance with court rulings, it was decided that citizens can display the crèche only if we mix it with a variety of other symbols that celebrate the "Winter Holiday." This would mean Santa, the reindeer, snowmen (or snowpersons) and a host of other frolicking replicas that have nothing to do with the true meaning of Christmas.

Furthermore, the annual Christmas musical put on by the children of our schools has been stripped of songs that have "religious content." They will, however, be able to play such tunes if they are instrumental renderings.

In celebration of this action by our city, I have come upon an alternative to a beloved Christmas song that children around the world enjoy at this time of year. I offer it in honor of the wise persons who have come up with this brilliant plan and hope the children of Hartville Elementary will be allowed to sing it during their program.

The song is entitled "Away With the Manger."

Away with the manger, we just don't have room,
We've got enough tinsel and big red costumes.
We'd like to hear music that goes with the day,
But if you sing words we'll make you go away.

We like all the snow and wreaths on the doors,
We love Christmas sales at department stores.
We want to rejoice in our good winter cheer,
So keep your religion, it's "X"mas this year.

Away with the manger, the menorah as well.
We love the old fat guy with presents to tell
The story of Christmas our culture holds dear,
To buy it on credit, no int'rest till next year.

Okay, you can have your display this year,
Just include a Frosty and all eight reindeer.
We'll put up a tree too, the rules we can bend,
We've got equal opportunity rights to offend.

Away with the manger, we've got a complaint,
Someone took issue with old Nick, that dear
    saint.
Be glad and be happy, you're not in the lurch,
You can sing of that baby next week in your
    church.

Signed,
Concerned in Hartville

I took one look at the letter and thought it was a gift
from the gods. Perfect! In a column just before
Thanksgiving I had agreed with the city fathers regarding the separation of church and state and
thought their solution was a good one. But this was

just too funny to risk losing in the great chasm known as "Letters to the Editor."

I quickly wrote some commentary around the letter and placed it in the bin on the desk of my boss, Betty Stanton.

Realize that Betty had not questioned a column of mine in at least two weeks—I think the last one had been the infamous stoplight installation piece. We don't see eye to eye on much of anything. Her life revolves around the paper and Elvis. She has one of those velvet wall hangings of the King in her office and a replica of his rhinestone-studded jumpsuit on her desk. Once I made a joke about Elvis' sideburns while he was still with us, and for a moment I thought I wasn't going to be. Betty's so devoted she made a pilgrimage to Graceland and brought back a signed copy of the single "Teddy Bear." She even calls her basement "the Jungle Room"—I've never had the nerve to actually visit.

Betty does respect my right to an opinion. She encourages my writing on controversial subjects, as long as they don't have anything to do with the King, thank you very much.

Later that day Betty walked into my office holding my column against her hip. She is not slight in stature. I could tell it was her by the great creaking of the concrete slab. Betty looked like a backhoe ready to tear the top off a condemned building.

"What is this?" she said.

"It's called a column, Betty. You know, about 750 words. They put that in the paper and people read it."

She was not amused.

"Where did you get the letter?"

"It was in the mail."

"Who's it from?"

"It wasn't signed."

I could tell she was pretty upset because she wasn't making small talk. Usually Betty beats around the bush with her conversation. Even if she were going to fire you, she'd start out by talking about how good the fruitcake was at the office party last year or offer you a peanut-butter ball, complete with the recipe. Underneath all those layers of Little Debbie cakes and Ho-Hos she keeps in her desk, she's a kind woman with a big heart.

But she wasn't in the mood for such conversation, and I'll admit I started questioning my judgment. I hadn't really thought about the piece that much. It had been reflex: I read, I laughed, I typed.

"What's the matter with it?" I said. "Some kind of legal problem?"

Betty took off her glasses with her free hand and let them dangle around her neck on their elastic cord. They're those black cat-eye glasses that went out of style about a hundred years ago, and I've wanted to take them off and crush them more than a few times. They left two blotches on her nose and crimson lines running straight back to her ears that looked like you could plant corn in them and get a pretty good crop.

The pupils of her eyes were as big as a pair of pine needles, and you would have thought by the way she looked at me that I had thrown her cat, Priscilla, in the blender and set it to purée.

"You know what people are going to say when they read this?" she said. Her chin, the top one, was all tight and puckered.

"I hope they laugh and say you ought to give me a raise, Betty."

She didn't return my smile.

"You're going to stir up more than you think if we print this."

"Aw, Betty, you're overdoing it. It's a letter. It's opinion. It's just a column. I've heard you say half the town takes the paper to make people think they can read and the other half only checks the obituaries to make sure they're not dead yet."

She put her glasses back on, and the blotches and lines disappeared.

"Don't say I didn't warn you," she said. I heard the sound of polyester in pain as she swished back down the hall. It was like the crunch of powdery snow beneath a size-15 pair of boots.

"Ladies and gentlemen, Betty has left the building," I said under my breath.

I guess if I'd known what was going to happen next, I would have listened to her.

THE PHONES

ily, Kelly and Brian are wonderful kids, but you wouldn't want to be around them after they've had sugared cereal. I usually try to get out of the house before the Honeycomb kicks in.

Lily is almost thirteen and learns more in the eighth grade than I did in college. She's cute, but she's also a teenager now and that scares me. Kelly is eleven and wants a horse. She tells me all her friends at school have horses, but I'm not convinced, particularly regarding her friends who live in Hartville Garden Apartments.

"Where do they keep them?" I say.

"Near the tennis courts?" she smiles.

Both are really good with Brian, age seven, and they give Evelyn and me a break every now and then.

My wife, Evelyn, is four years my senior and is sometimes mistaken for my daughter. She looks like she's twenty, exercises, gets lots of rest and at breakfast eats a mixture of puffed wheat and Sandpaper Bran. At least that's what it looks like. She can't stand that I buy the kids the sweet stuff, but it makes them happy, and I feel I do that all too seldom.

As I walk out the door I sometimes hear them say, "Can't Daddy pour our cereal?" If I'm out of the house by 7:30 I avoid the onslaught. I try for quality time, but breakfast isn't quality.

That morning, however, the morning of the column's appearance, I awoke to a strange ringing sensation. It seemed I was floating above myself with a sweet jangling of festive bells, the turkey smell still hanging heavy in the air.

Some people say they dream in color, with every hue and tone in perfect symmetry. They speak of recurring scenes of falling off cliffs or walking on clouds. But I dream in sentences, sometimes complete, sometimes fragments, and I wake with commas and apostrophes floating through my mind. My life is words, and words never sleep. They wait for me, like an old dog curled on the throw rug, tail beating. Words wait and wake me, and spend nights near my lips until they can work their way through my fingers onto a page.

I finally pried my eyes open to see 6:15 on the alarm. A word came to me I will not let escape here. Bad word. Then I heard the sound again—not the bells of St. Mary's as I had originally thought, but the telephone.

Terrible things happen when people call you at 6:15 a.m. You're late for something, or it's a death in the family, or it might be D.J. Starr, which is ten times worse.

"Hello," I said, giving it my best shot to sound awake. I don't know why I try to impress people by trying not to sound like I've just awakened, but I do.

"Jackson Grim, this is D.J. Starr at Hartville Radio and you're on the air!"

In my opinion, morning radio is the gasoline that fuels pop culture. It is dumbing down via the ionosphere. Cultural pollution transmitted unseen to car stereos, headsets and clock radios. Driven by insipid music, screaming commercials and obnoxious hosts who love to air their disagreements with management, morning radio is the equivalent of an audio Twinkie. It is art laced with MSG with a side of fries, hush puppies and heavily salted opinion. Listeners are dragged through every Hollywood scandal, lurid stories about political leaders and a cacophony of callers who start each sentence with "I just love your show."

Every morning program has someone named Buck, D. J. or Starr. Hartville has two out of three in one person. His real name is Carlin Hardwell. He has worked for sixteen stations in the last fifteen years. They are broadcasting giants in places like Mammoth, Colorado; Pittsfield, Iowa; Tarmac, Minnesota; and Platteville, Wisconsin. D.J.'s frequent live calls to unsuspecting victims are illegal. The lawyers keep telling him that, but he keeps it up because "it's good radio."

D.J. can best be described by the word *annoying*. His voice is annoying. His jokes are annoying. The music he plays is annoying. But just about everybody listens to him at some point in the morning, particularly kids who want to hear the school lunch menu or if there's a closing because of a big snow. For a print guy it's enough to make what little hair I have left stand on end.

D.J.'s shelf life is about eight months to a year in most towns, since it takes about that much time to go through his sound-effects carts and spoof songs. He had been in Hartville about six months when I got the call.

"Hello, D.J.," I said in a fog. "What can I do for you?"

"Well, I hope we're not waking you up, but we just had to comment on your column about the song."

I was surprised he'd finished the comics that early.

"Well, it kind of speaks for itself," I said.

"Now, was this an actual letter delivered to you, or did you come up with it and attribute it to a reader?"

"It was an actual letter, D.J."

A tinny squeak was coming from the phone, because D.J. turns his headphones to an eardrum-splitting level that no one on the planet can stand other than morning show hosts. Radio people naturally like everything loud, particularly when it's their own voice. When D.J. talks off the air he speaks like he's listening to a CD on maximum level, but there is no volume control for him.

D.J. read the poem, and I tried to get out as gracefully as I could. I thanked him for mentioning the story and encouraged people to pick up an extra copy of the paper for family members. I figured Betty would appreciate the plug. I tried to humor him and profusely thanked him for the call, but before I could get off the phone D.J. interrupted me.

"Go ahead, caller," D.J. said.

"Hello? Am I on?"

"Yes, go ahead!"

"My name is Harold Whinnel, from over on Pine Bluff, and if the words to that song weren't so true I'd be laughing right along with you."

"What do you mean, Harold? You pretty upset about the city council, huh?" D.J. said.

"You bet I am—I mean, I don't bet—I mean, yessir I'm upset. The first thing they do is put an *X* for

214

Christmas and then they take away our manger. Next they'll be coming for our churches, telling us we can't read the Bible."

"I don't think that's what the council . . ." I said, coming out of the fog, but D.J. cut me off again.

"Well, it looks like a lot of you have opinions on this one, because the phone lines are jammed."

There is an axiom in radio that a person's voice *never* matches a person's looks. Most people had never seen D.J. or the inner workings of the station. When he said, "The phone lines are jammed," listeners thought of a control board with a maze of buttons and flashing lights that would scare an air-traffic controller. In their minds D.J. was about thirty-five with short, brown hair, maybe a mustache, 6'2", trim and clean-shaven.

But I had been to the station. I had seen D.J. I knew what was happening. D.J. was just a tad under 5'4" with a goatlike beard he constantly stroked. His face was round like a gnome's, and his fingers were stubby and yellow from nicotine. An overflowing ashtray sat at his side, and wire copy was piled on the turntables beside him. The station still hadn't sprung for a CD player and just barely had enough money to keep the tape machine heads cleaned.

The "jammed phone lines" were exactly two lights that blinked haphazardly by D.J.'s side. There was only one on-air phone line hooked into the control board, so to get response from callers other than the guest D.J. hit the speakerphone in front of him and grabbed a coat hanger suspended from the ceiling. At the end of the hanger, gray electrical tape secured a dented Electrovoice microphone. In my mind I could see him bend the hanger with a jerk, ashes scattering. I heard his headphones squeal again as he pushed the button for another call.

"Yeah, what do you think?"

"Am I on?"

"Yeah, this is Hartville Radio, go ahead."

Larry King had nothing to worry about.

"This all started when they took prayer and the Ten Commandments out of the schools."

"How's that?" D.J. said.

"Well, this is the effect. We can't even celebrate Christmas without worrying about being politically correct. Jesus is the reason for the season. It's as simple as that."

I tried to respond, but D.J. was having too much fun egging the callers on. He hung up and immediately punched in another, who pointed blame a little closer to home.

"The guy you have on there right now is part of the problem, D.J. He's part of the media elite that wants to set their agenda, and if it wasn't for programs like yours, we probably wouldn't hear a thing about what's going on at City Hall."

I don't think I'm part of the media elite. I worked my way through Hartville College and eked out a journalism degree. After an internship at the paper

I started beat reporting and finally graduated to the column. I basically do that and whatever else Betty assigns to me. Don't get me wrong. I'm not saying I'm a conservative, but Dan Rather and I don't do lunch every month to plot our next stack of biased stories. It just doesn't happen.

I tried to explain, but D.J. just kept taking more calls. It was like throwing lighter fluid into a fireplace. The flames grew hotter, the voices licked higher on the air, and I was getting sick. It was morning radio at its best, or worst, depending on your point of view.

The conservatives in Hartville had been quiet, almost subdued, in their reaction to the council's decision. The evil in the culture was so great, it seemed they were resigned to watch passively. But the column sparked something. Like a rushing underground current, the Christians suddenly rose to the surface and took the rest of Hartville with them.

That afternoon the phone rang. And rang. And rang. Betty swished by and gave me the "I told you so" look, though she never actually said it.

Mostly the callers were fundamentalists upset about the direction of the country and particularly the way the City Council and the media were X-ing Christ out of Christmas. I responded by saying I was the one who had printed the letter; if I was biased, why would I have let it go through? The logic didn't work. Most felt it was a fluke, that a story had gotten by the gatekeeper, which it had.

It was curious to me that the religious community was angry with the culture they had retreated from so many years earlier. They had constructed their own Christian ghetto inside America with Christian bookstores, Christian radio stations, Christian workout videos, Christian recording artists, Christian comedians, Christian T-shirts, Christian antioxidants and Christian aluminum siding complete with fish symbols.

Around two o'clock my ear was red and stinging from all the calls. I picked up the phone on the first ring and said, "I know you're angry about the culture and Jesus is the reason for the season. Okay?"

"Mr. Grim?"

"Yes."

"This is Pastor Marty Karlsen at Hartville Community Church, and I just want to thank you for printing the letter this morning."

"You do?"

"Yes, I think you've done a great service to the Christian community in this town. There are some of us who are too lily-livered to take a stand for the faith, and you've helped galvanize us."

Karlsen talked with a slight drawl, like he was a transplant from the South, which was weird because he was actually Swedish. I imagined him putting barbecue sauce on his lutefisk. His voice was low and gravelly, with a tremolo that bleated occasionally, somewhat like Mr. Haney on *Green Acres*. I assumed he was probably good at what he did, stirring people up and reassuring them that they were on the path to heaven, though religion isn't my thing.

"I did all that?" I said.

"We won't know the entire effect until the school board meeting next week, but I'd say your writing, though you haven't always been a friend of our cause, has helped a great deal. That's unusual because of the liberal bias I know you have, but still there's reason to rejoice."

"What's supposed to happen at the school board meeting?" I said, intentionally ignoring the bias comment.

"Our public schools have abandoned the historic Judeo-Christian tradition. Secular humanists have taken over, and the multiculturalists of the day have changed the curriculum from reading, writing and arithmetic to classes in womyn's studies and whole language and outcome-based education and inventive spelling . . ."

I checked out just after the secular humanism quote and put it on autopilot, because I had heard the same thing all morning and even at lunch. All I wanted was a ham sandwich from the deli, but I couldn't get to the counter without someone stepping in front and saying, "You're that column guy, aren't you?" These people were everywhere.

"So during the school board meeting," Marty said as I checked back in, "a group of concerned citizens will give their views about the content of the new

Winter Celebration at the school. We're praying it's going to be a victory for all Bible-believing Christians in Hartville and hopefully throughout the United States!"

I let my answering machine pick up the calls for an hour or so while I composed my column for the next day. It wasn't hard to choose a topic. I took excerpts from conversations, most of them angry at media attitudes toward Christians and the truth of the song I had printed.

I received one call from Dierdra Bergman Freep, who said she was appalled that I would "turn to religion to sell papers."

"These crazy, wacko fundamentalists think God gave them the right to run everybody's life. They want to elect a preacher as president and run the country from their churches."

The previous year Dierdra's group, Atheists Against Mangers, had singlehandedly wrenched the manger from the lawn of City Hall. A.A.M. was small, but when you use a lawyer's stationery to correspond with the city, people pay attention. When the council discovered a legal precedent called the "reindeer rule," Jesus returned, sharing the space with Frosty and Rudolph.

"These people need to get over their love affair with the manger," Dierdra had said. "They're followers, like sheep, mostly lower-class, uneducated and easy to lead. Religion is in their DNA."

The town had gone into a general state of shock after that statement. Many of the religious folk had protested, but most just shook their heads and figured they couldn't do anything to stop her.

So I finished the article while listening to my answering machine click and beep and wheeze. It finally sputtered and gave up the tape. It was sad watching it spin its final bit of oxide across the playhead, but I guess we're all appointed a certain number of days on this earth. I wasn't sure how people would react to the second column, but I felt it was the least I could do in tribute to the fallen machine.

The next day I found out D.J. had done his homework. After my call on the morning show, he had challenged others in town to come up with their own songs and audition to sing them on the air.

Being sensitive to the townsfolk, I would describe Hartville as musically challenged. We have no center for performing arts. There is no Hartville orchestra. The Barbershop Quartet Society left town because they couldn't find four people who could sing in the same key.

But with all those strikes against them, the people of Hartville rose to the occasion. I guess hell hath no fury like an angry Christian with a guitar.

Betty taped the whole program the next morning and gave it to me on two cassettes. Here's a portion of the transcript of the songs from the broadcast.

D.J.:   All right, our first presentation will be some gentlemen from—where was it again?

BASS VOICE: Hartville Community Church. We're the men's quartet.

D.J.:   And all three of you are a part of that?

TENOR VOICE: Yes sir.

D.J.:   Where's the fourth guy?

BASS VOICE: We don't have a fourth guy.

D.J.:   Then how can you be a quartet?

BASS VOICE: The church already had a men's trio.

D.J.:   I see. So the quartet is going to sing what?

BASS VOICE: This is our version of "Good Christian Men, Rejoice."

D.J.:   And what is that one about?

BASS VOICE: The original was a song proclaiming the good news that Jesus was born, but this version is called "Good Secular Men, Rejoice."

D.J.:   Well, [squeal] I'm sure we'll all catch on. Get up to the microphone there so we can all hear you.

(There are muffled sounds of rattling paper and general confusion of the quartet until the discordant strum of a guitar is heard, along with the a cappella harmony of three men lumbering around the melody.)

Good secular men, rejoice
With heart and soul and voice.
Give ye heed to what we say: News! News!
Don't sing your Christmas song today.
Sing of reindeers and of Claus,
Just don't say "Jesus" now because
We'll be sued today, we'll be sued today.

Good liberal men, with zest
Hire lawyers to protest.
File briefs aplenty and with flair: Bill! Bill!
Christ isn't for the public square.
Play tunes by Springsteen and John Tesh,
Tear down our dear old Christmas crèche,
File a suit today, file a suit today.

Good libbers, we won't leave you out.
We don't want you to scream and shout.
Religion is for all those men: Pigs! Pigs!
Who oppress the good womyn.
You want equal time to pray
To god your Mother? This we say,
"You are not correct, you are not correct."

Revisionists, this is our last verse.
No need to clamor or to curse.
The Bible it is full of flaws: Revise! Revise!
Strike out the miracles because
They can't be true; you want to pray
To the Eternal It today?

Thanks, but no thanks; thanks, but no thanks.

D.J.:   Hey, I've heard that one before, and you guys are pretty good, huh?

FEMALE VOICE: [applause and giggles] Really good, D.J.

BASS VOICE: And we'd like to invite everybody to the church this Sunday . . .

D.J.:   Yeah, yeah, that's great. Now we've got somebody else here— thank you, boys.

FEMALE VOICE: Hi, D.J.

D.J.:   And you must be Jenny Logan, right?

JENNY: That's right, I'm home-schooled with my three brothers and sisters, and we're learning a lot about the history of Christmas hymns this year.

D.J.:   Okay, and what are you going to sing?

JENNY: We chose one of people's favorite Christmas songs, "Silent Night."

D.J.:   Yeah, I think everybody likes that one.

JENNY: But in this version, it's kind of like a parody, you know? Well, I sing a song Franz Gruber never thought of. He was the German guy who didn't know any better and put in

	all those politically incorrect words like *holy, Savior* and *heaven.* I've come up with a version that won't offend so many people as kind of a commentary on modern society.
D.J.:	And how old are you?
JENNY:	Twelve.
D.J.:	Wow! When I was twelve I couldn't even pronounce half the words you just used. Is that a cassette player you have there?
JENNY:	Yes, my mom played the organ at church, and we recorded it. And just so you know, my mom wrote the last verse especially for our family.
D.J.:	All right, ladies and jellyfish, here she is, the beautiful Jenny Logan with her "Silent Night," the P.C. version.

Silent night, Solstice night,
All is calm, all half price.
Round yon department store, all of us strangers,
Wondering who will get the last Power Rangers,
Shop in heavenly peace, shop in heavenly peace.

Silent night, wonderful night,
All the house filled with light.

Round the windows, shrubs and flowerpots,
Blinking lights, burning thousands of watts:
Sleep with blindfolds on, sleep with blindfolds on.

Silent night, Christmas night,
All the toys out of sight.
Dad in his nightshirt and me with my caps
Trudge up to bed, and then we collapse.
There has got to be more. Surely there's something more.

Another highlight of the broadcast was an a cappella version of "Away With the Manger" sung by D.J. himself.

I thought the whole thing might die down with everybody making fun of the situation. But it didn't. Things got worse.

RUDOLPH
THE NOSELESS
REINDEER

anta has never been a militant figure to me. He's always been kind of cute and cuddly with the presents, round belly and reindeer. But to the religious right in town, he's the worst. Switch a couple of letters around in his name and you get Satan. He's that bad.

Santa made his incarnations at several retailers in town. Mostly he was ringing bells outside the grocery and department stores. But the St. Nicks of Hartville appeared to have eating disorders. They were thin, with beards that hung in clumps, and they wore badly faded red suits and black coverings over tennis shoes that no one but true believers thought were boots.

It was the first Monday in December, and the school board meeting was two days away. You could feel the tension in the air. People were still talking about D.J.'s program and my column. In a small town you tend to cling to such things.

The anti-Christmas contingent was on the sideline, gloating over all the furor. They had won in the courts. The law was on their side. And they had Dierdra Bergman Freep as their spokesperson, which created a sense of resolve and contentment in the ranks.

But the Christians were slowly organizing their troops. Pastor Karlsen was busy recording his daily fifteen-minute radio program for the local Christian station. The original name of the program had been *The Freedom Hour*. When they realized the incongruity of the program's title and length, though, they changed it to *Heart to Hartville*. The station really didn't have an opinion since it would be paid no matter what the name, so they aired it every day at 10:00 a.m., right after the farm report.

The format of the program consisted of the announcer, Deacon Immer Wright, talking over an ancient recording of Squire Parson's "Beulah Land." Deacon Wright owned Wright's Hardware, the current site of the Christmas crèche. He had it displayed on the sidewalk in front of his store, and when anyone of like mind passed, they honked and the deacon would appear inside the window in front of the "Jesus Is the Reason for the Season" banner.

Deacon Wright did not have an announcer's voice, but like D.J. he loved to hear it, whether it was during a prayer meeting or on the radio. And since he underwrote half the cost of the show's airtime, he'd made the strong suggestion that he introduce the pastor at the start of each program. No one on the church board objected.

Deacon Wright always ended his introduction with "And now, from our heart to yours, here's the pastor of Hartville Community Church, Marty Karlsen."

With "Beulah Land" swelling in the background, Pastor Karlsen would begin his Bible study. When he was finished, Deacon Wright would return with announcements and the closing theme, more "Beulah Land."

On this Monday, Karlsen introduced a series of programs he called "Turning Back the Night" to mobilize stealth Christians who would denounce the secularization of the Christmas holiday. The program was so special that they had decided to change the theme of the show to "Onward Christian Soldiers." This put pressure on the deacon: it was live, it was different, and it confused him to no end. It had taken months for him to memorize his opening lines.

The broadcast began with music, then the deacon said, "Welcome to *Heart to Hartville,* a daily broadcast of inspiration and encouragement that . . . uh . . . helps you turn back the night . . ."

"Onward Christian soldiers, marching as to war . . ."

"And now, from the heart . . . of . . . ours to yours, here's Pastor Karlsen. [barely audible] I told you we should have recorded it, Marty."

Karlsen commended those who took their faith seriously and urged listeners to "exercise their God-given right to speak out against the darkness." He was referring to the Wednesday-night school board meeting, of course, but as he spoke an idea began forming in the brain of Deacon Wright. When the pastor finished two minutes early, concluding with "They have perverted everything they've put their slimy hands on. We need to put the devil in his place and the secular humanists with him," the door was open for a move of the Spirit.

"I feel in my heart," Deacon Wright said, "that we ought to seize this opportunity to really show these people we mean business."

The recording room was situated behind the main studio of the radio station, with nothing between but double-paned glass. The operator on duty later told me he glanced back just as the deacon began his speech and saw Marty Karlsen's eyes "wide as the south end of a northbound elephant."

"I have some posters and wood at the hardware store that I'd like to donate to anyone who will put their feet where their mouth is and walk around City Hall to show we mean what we say."

If you listen closely to the tape, you'll hear Pastor Karlsen clear his throat repeatedly, increasingly closer to the microphone.

"And I say this afternoon is the perfect time to put your faith into action. [Ahem] We need creative people who can print placards and think up catchy sayings and more people to walk around City Hall. [AHEM]"

". . . With the cross of Jesus, going on before."

The city building, just a block from Hartville's main shopping area, is arguably the prettiest structure in the county. It was built fifty years ago with huge stones from a nearby quarry, so it is marked by a stateliness, elegance and charm that will continue long after this generation leaves the planet.

The lawn in front of City Hall sports several oaks; two huge cedars are positioned strategically at the entrance. In November and December the lights on the trees reflect from the glass in the hall, giving a double illumination effect. When there is a light coating of snow on the ground, you'll often see children playing on the undulating lawn. Families pose for holiday newsletter pictures.

To the dismay of Christians, City Hall's dignity is marred by an ungainly appendage between Thanksgiving and Christmas each year. A red trailer is chained to a parking meter on the east side of City Hall. A sign hanging slightly askew says

"Santa's Workshop." Children are brought into the dimly lit room, most of them wailing and kicking, and have their picture taken with another bony Santa. This of course is an exercise for the parents, not the children, and Santa does a brisk business in Hartville.

A small gray speaker mounted on top of the trailer plays a tinny "Rudolph" by Gene Autry and the Peanuts theme by Vince Guaraldi. Every thirty seconds Mrs. Santa invites the "kiddies" waiting outside to think hard about what they want her husband to bring them this year. On this fateful night Mrs. Santa was in rare form.

Not far away, about fifty people huddled together in front of City Hall with signs that read "Jesus Is the Reason for the Season," "Put Christ Back in Christmas" and "Santa Didn't Die for Your Sins!" The sun was nearly finished for the day, and shoppers scurried along with their bags. A line about fifteen deep formed in front of Santa's place as parents tried to beat closing time.

Deacon Wright, a former marine, and looking somewhat like Bull Conner at a civil rights march, led the way, encouraging his followers by chanting, "You can't take our holiday!"

They repeated in unison, "You can't take our holiday!"

"It's in our heart and here to stay!"

"Sound off, Jesus!"

"Sound off, he's born!"

There are conflicting reports about how the fight began. Some say one of the elves asked the marchers to lower the volume of their singing. Others contend it was the nasally sound of Gene Autry that pushed the protesters over the brink. Whatever it was, the next day the headline on the front of the *Daily News* said, "Police Arrest Four in Skirmish with Santa."

Christmas is supposed to bring peace on earth, goodwill to men, but just the opposite happened at City Hall last night.

Four protesters were arrested, then released after allegedly attacking Santa Claus at his holiday workshop. One elf was also slightly injured.

About 50 people holding banners and singing Christmas songs criticized the recent decision concerning the presence of a manger scene on government property. The fight broke out shortly after 5:30 p.m.

"We were just minding our own business, taking pictures with the kids, when those people showed up," said the elf, who requested anonymity. "It was awful. They broke the nose off of Rudolph and nearly killed Santa."

Immer Wright, owner of Wright's Hardware and deacon at Hartville Community Church, was involved in the melee.

"I don't really know what started it," Wright said. "All I know is that we've got the right to protest just as much as they have the right to merchandise a sacred holiday."

A shaken Santa refused to file charges against the group, saying he did not want to reveal his identity. The red-suited man was so upset by the ordeal that he asked the children in line to return Tuesday for complimentary photos and visits.

The incident comes in the wake of public outcry spurred by columnist Jackson Grim, who included a politically correct Christmas Hymn in his column, and it comes two days prior to a school board meeting where citizens are expected to turn out in record numbers.

Marty Karlsen, pastor of Hartville Community Church, where many of the protesters attend, said he was distressed about the outbreak of violence over the issue.

"Many people in our congregation feel very strongly about celebrating Christmas the right way," Karlsen said. "We certainly don't condone violence, and if I were to talk with Santa, or the man who was playing Santa—of course we all know he wasn't the real . . . I mean, well, if I could speak to whoever it was underneath that fake beard and red suit, I would ask him to reconsider the perpetration of a lie to the children of this community. We would, of course, like to help him repair his reindeer if that can be done.

"That doesn't mean we're pro-Santa," he added. "We're just pro-people, no matter who they dress up as."

When I read the article Tuesday morning, I wondered what Dierdra Bergman Freep was thinking. I figured she would show up at the Wednesday meeting with her sons, Tim and Rob. And I figured this was one school board meeting I couldn't afford to miss.

GOD IN THE
SNOWBANK

hristmas always brings out
the best in people. That's what
I've heard, but don't believe
it. The truth is, Christmas
should bring out the best in
people, but it doesn't.

There are always the
niceties of fruitcake and gift
fudge sent by relatives who
have no business making either. There's an occasional smile amidst the scramble for the last over-
priced action figure or hot doll of the season.

But most people live in their own world at
Christmas, in a hurry and looking for presents that
might make them feel they haven't blown it this
year. Especially men. Christmas brings to all males
a deep need to be satisfied, for love and warmth. A
man wants to please his wife and kids, but

Christmas expectations hang over him like an overgrown evergreen. The tree that looks so bright and healthy in December eventually drops needles on the carpet which are discovered around March, when he's barefoot and least expecting it.

Christmas is an endless winter of expectations. The child thinks, *I hope I don't get clothes,* while the parent thinks, *She's really going to like the turtleneck and leggings.* The mother ponders all the possibilities. *I just don't want him to put it off and spend too much,* she says to herself, while the husband thinks, *Next year I'm not going to put it off and spend so much, but at least she'll be happy with this rhinestone hair dryer.*

The husband then focuses on himself. After a harrowing evening of traffic, zigzagging through endless hordes of equally clueless husbands, he muses, *Just once, just one Christmas, may it not be a tie. Or a sweater. Or a book that someone else wanted to read—someone who hopes you'll leave it lying around so they can pick it up. Just once let it be something that makes me feel like a child again.*

But Christmas can never make you feel like a child unless you are ready for it. The busyness and the lists and the expectations crowd the day. We fall over ourselves hanging happiness on the eaves and plastering joy on the wall, and still Christmas ends and we wonder what happened. Broken joy can't be replaced like Christmas lights.

This is what Christmas meant to me that year. Between Thanksgiving and the 25th of December, I checked out. I was there when we trimmed the tree and opened the presents, but not all there. Christmases past had taught me to hold back. I laughed at the delight of the kids and their excitement when they tore into the gifts, but deep down it was like watching someone root for the Chicago Cubs or the Boston Red Sox, who never win. You had to feel sorry for the little saps. They just didn't get it.

You can't win at Christmas. You can't ever really have joy because there's something staring you in the face called LIFE, and I don't mean the magazine. Life is there with its hopes and dreams like ornaments on the tree. After years of life, you realize these ornaments aren't real. You pick them off a week after the big day and wrap the dreams in paper. You stuff hope in a dusty box and shove it in a closet until next year, when you're a little older and a little closer to being recycled like the tree in the living room.

Man, Christmas is just downright depressing!

It helped that I was in the middle of the hullabaloo about the "Away With the Manger" column. People in town who had never noticed me before came up and patted me on the back and said, "Hey, Jackson, hey, you're the one that wrote that column, aren't you?" And I would say, "Yes I am," and they would smile and say, "Hey, that column was something else." And then they would laugh or just stare at me as if they could look into my eyes and see another column growing somewhere between my cornea and brain. Or they would scuff at the ground with one foot and grin uncomfortably, not knowing what to do. So I'd say I needed to go to the grocery to pick up a cantaloupe and that usually got me out of there.

But underneath all the activity was an emptiness and a sense that I was in big trouble. *We* were in big trouble. The whole town was sitting on a powder keg, antsy for something to happen, and it affected everyone's mental state.

Again, it showed up on the air.

Calls were coming in to the program *Your Turn* on Hartville Radio. A snowdrift closed down one of the main roads, and, as happens in small towns, weather became news. It was as if we'd never seen snow before. *Your Turn's* host, Darby Gardner, at some point in his life had taught sociology at a junior college. We picked that up because he would mention it about every five minutes. He now sold insurance and gave advice on mutual funds that he just happened to sell at a pretty good commission, but the love of his life was *Your Turn*. It was his gift to Hartville.

"It's *Your Turn,* with Darby Gardner," the announcer would say, quickly followed by swelling music that reminded me of the *Captain Kangaroo* theme. "Now, heeeeeeeere's Darby."

On the news prior to the show the road closing was the top story, closely followed by the school board meeting, with a veiled reference to my column. When Darby gave his introduction for the evening's topic, he said it had taken him twice as long as usual to get to the studio because of the snowdrift. Then he added that the wind had blown the snow into such a strange shape that it took on a ghostly effect and he couldn't get it out of his mind.

The school board meeting led Darby's list of gripes. It had been the main topic for the past three nights, but a caller jumped on the snowdrift reference immediately. The voice was a bit quavery, and I imagined a rotary dial, a wrinkled face and skin underneath her arms hanging like the wattle of a turkey.

CALLER 1: Darby, I saw the same thing on the news, and I was wondering if anyone else noticed it. I'm glad you mentioned it.

DARBY: And what was it you saw?

CALLER 1: It looked like an angel to me. The angel Gabriel maybe. You could see its wings up by the interstate overpass and then down at the bottom the face. Did you see that?

DARBY: Well, no, I can't say that I perceived anything angelic about it, but let's find out if anyone agrees with you. Hello?

CALLER 2: Yeah, I saw it, only I didn't see no angel.

DARBY: You were driving there?

CALLER 2: I went by it on the way to the store. Now I'm not a religious nut, and I haven't been into this manger thing that much, but it looked to me like those pictures of Jesus we used to take home from Sunday school when we were kids. I could see the beard and the long hair and everything.

DARBY: Very interesting—so there seems to be a religious element to the sightings so far. Thank you. Yes, you're on the air.

CALLER 3: Yeah, hi, Darby. I seen it on the news and it looked to me like it was a possum in the middle with its tail wrapped around a limb, then over in the right corner there was a militarylike person hunched over and eating a can of Spam.

DARBY: Well, that's a new one. I can't say I saw that. Let's take another and see if anyone else thinks they see something.

CALLER 4: Love your show, Darby.

DARBY: Thank you.

CALLER 4: I think it looks like, and I'm not saying it was actually him, but I think it looks like Uncle Jed from the *Beverly Hillbillies.*

DARBY: Interesting that you would use the name of the character on that program instead of Buddy Ebsen. There was a study not too long ago that looked at the sociological significance of the media's influence

241

on culture. I used to teach a class that dealt with some of those issues and . . .

CALLER 4: Well, I don't know about that, but it looked like Uncle Jed to me. That's all I'm saying.

DARBY: All right, yes, one more then.

CALLER 5: I saw the one that lady was talking about.

DARBY: Buddy Ebsen?

CALLER 5: No, the one that looked like Jesus in the takehome papers. I think with all that's going on in this town, we're getting a sign from God!

This went on for quite some time, with people seeing everything in the snow from the Holy Grail to General Custer. But overwhelmingly people said they saw Jesus, the manger, the wise men or a member of the Holy Family.

They were still talking the next night when half the town met in the school gymnasium, and for many the image had changed in the interim. The person who had said she saw the possum called D.J. in the morning and swore it now looked like Elvis Presley in Blue Hawaii. I suspected Betty, of course. I sat near the front right, behind Dierdra Bergman Freep and her contingent from Atheists Against Mangers.

No matter what you think of her, Dierdra is an interesting character. I had written a feature story about her when she first reared her atheistic head in public. She seemed to like the publicity, though she looked with suspicion at the questions I asked. When I tried to find out more about her personal side, she refused to answer, and I had to rely on secondary sources who lived in her old hometown. I didn't put those findings in the story, but much of it made sense.

Dierdra had not always been antagonistic to religion. In fact, she was raised attending church, but an abusive father and teenage rebellion sent her away—at least that's what the sources said. The final straw came when Dierdra's husband, who was heavily involved in a church, abandoned her after Rob was born, leaving her with nothing but a mortgage and two fatherless boys. That was when she went back to her maiden name and took on a look that would frighten a defensive lineman. I suspect most people in Hartville who hated Dierdra for her stand would have been kinder had they known her situation.

Behind me several churchgoers commented on the broadcast and made references to "those people," who sat only a couple of rows away. A journalist/columnist always likes to be in the middle of a story, but I'll admit it seemed a little too close for comfort.

The school board, accustomed to a small room with no audience, timidly made its way to the long table with a microphone at each seat. Cameras from the local television station were there, and several members shielded their eyes from the harsh lights as they were seated. They looked like sacrificial lambs heading for the altar.

When Jeannette Harris, head of the board, asked us to stand for the Pledge of Allegiance, I heard Dierdra say, "Here we go." The following is my ear-witness account.

"I pledge allegiance to the flag [cough] the United States of America. [Louder cough] And to the republic, for which it stands. [Several coughs] One nation, under [A COUGH CRESCENDO], indivisible, with liberty and justice for all."

Both of Dierdra's sons were with her that evening. Tim was eight and in the third grade. Already his shoulders sagged from two years of teasing and derision from other kids. You can imagine what a last name like Freep will do to a child. On top of that, the leading atheist in town was his mother. The word that comes to mind when I think of Tim is *reluctant*. His life was like a video game with no controls. He could only sit and watch.

His brother, Rob, was four and had not yet been exposed to the cruelty of others. He sat quietly for the first few minutes, then got out of his chair and ran around the gymnasium the rest of the night. I think one of the TV people gave him a lens cap to play with so he wouldn't trip over their cables, and he used it as a Frisbee throughout the proceedings.

Jeannette Harris took control of the meeting and explained that they would give as many as possible a chance to voice their opinion. The subject was the school's annual "Winter Celebration," and they would take comments from parents immediately after the old business.

The old business had gone nearly forty-five minutes when Dierdra stood up and yelled, "You can stop stalling and get to it, because I'm not going home until I have my say."

This brought a general round of applause from the crowd, and I believe it may have been the first time the two sides had agreed on anything. Jeannette closed one book and opened another on the table. Carl Luntgren, a toadish-looking man with little hair and much girth, motioned for new business, and immediately people lined up behind the single microphone in the center aisle, just behind the free-throw line. A lens cap sailed by my head. Rob followed not far behind.

A young woman of about thirty was the first to speak. She had blond hair and wore a loose-fitting blouse and jeans that said she was practical rather than fashion-conscious. She had a rich alto voice that reverberated to the back of the gym and forward again.

"My name is Cheryl Fortney, and I have three children who attend Hartville Elementary. When I was a child I walked these same halls and even had some of the same teachers my children have."

She was reading from note cards stacked in her hand. Soon, however, she pushed them together and held them behind her back.

"I'm a Christian," she said determinedly. "And Christmas is a very special holiday for me and my family. I think the majority of people feel this way in our community. And for you to strike out the very meaning of Christmas from the songs and activities of our children is just plain wrong.

"Two of my children are in the musical this year, and when they showed me what they were allowed to sing, it just broke my heart. There was no 'Joy to the World,' no 'Hark the Herald Angels Sing.' There was Frosty and Rudolph and 'Here Comes Santa Claus,' but no mention of the reason we celebrate.

"I understand there are people in this community who don't believe in Jesus. Well, I don't believe in Santa or Rudolph, but I don't bar those songs. Why can't we have traditional Christmas carols included? What are we so afraid of?"

"If you'll recall," Carl Luntgren said, shifting in his folding chair, "the kids are singing 'Silent Night,' and last I heard that was a Christmas song."

Dierdra applauded, and her group followed along after she gave them a stern look.

"But they aren't allowed to sing it," Cheryl said. "They were told they had to hum it along with the instruments while one child read about the meaning of Kwanzaa."

Murmurs of disdain filtered through the audience. Carl shifted again, the chair squeaking painfully as if the rivets were about to pop.

"We appreciate your opinion," Jeannette said. "May we have the next, please?"

A tall, thin man stepped to the microphone and leaned down. He tapped it with his finger, then blew into it. His work clothes were soiled and hung on him like sheets on a clothesline. There was a halting drawl to his voice, and he chewed his words like tobacco.

"I'm Randy Cline. I live just over on Sycamore, and we've got two kids who go here. I don't understand how we can justify taking God out of the schools and putting in clinics that give out . . . well, that give out things we wouldn't even think of talking about a few years ago. You've taken down the Ten Commandments. You've said our kids can't pray in school. In one school they put a bag over a picture of Jesus until the Supreme Court said they had to take the whole thing down. And now you're taking Christmas away from us. That ain't right."

Most of the crowd roared in approval and applauded until Jeannette Harris banged the table and called for order.

"I just don't understand what we're coming to," Randy continued. "Our money says 'In God We Trust'; our pledge says 'one nation under God,' if you could hear it over the coughs tonight. We were founded as a Christian nation. And if you want to clean up the violence and gangs and all the problems we have, you ought not kick God out of the classroom but welcome him back in. That's all I have to say."

There was more applause as Randy stepped out of the way. He slid back into the sea of faces as Dierdra Bergman Freep grabbed the microphone and pushed the others out of the way.

"Right here is the problem the board has already addressed and addressed correctly," Dierdra said. "These fundamentalist Christians want everything their way, and when they don't get their way they try to impose their values on the rest of us. This school is for my boys. This school is for all the children of Hartville, not just Christians. There are Jews and Muslims and atheists and all kinds of people represented here, and the courts of our land have spoken. The government should not endorse a religion."

The applause was replaced by a low boo and a few hisses, but Dierdra's voice cut through the noise.

"Christianity has been responsible for more persecution and atrocities over the centuries than any other belief system. They believe in a virgin birth and a three-headed God and other wacky things that I don't even want my children exposed to, let alone made to believe. If they want to check out intellectually from this society and go to some hillside and live in caves, that's fine with me. But speaking for our society and others who are concerned about true freedom, a public school is no place to be advancing religion, so I would ask that if you have to have a program, you keep the Winter Celebration the way it is."

Another chorus of boos filled the room as Dierdra passed the gauntlet of jeering parents. She fed off their hatred. Her steps became more resolute, and by the time she got back to her chair she was smiling and laughing.

"Put that in your column, Grim," she said to me.

Another highlight of the meeting occurred when a short, well-dressed man came in through the side door. He wore designer gloves, a designer trench coat and designer shoes. The man at the microphone seemed to recognize him and stepped aside in favor of the new arrival. His gait was every bit as determined as Dierdra's, and we all knew he was a lawyer from the moment he banged on the outside door that said "No Entrance." He seemed like the type of man who would tell you how many times he had been before the Supreme Court and would do just about anything to get back there.

"My name is Hewitt Lawrence III, from Lawrence, Packer and Davidovic in Washington, D.C."

He spoke with every inch of his body, rising on his toes when he said important words and making eye contact with each board member.

"We are very concerned about what's going on in this school, and we are pursuing legal action in ac-

249

cordance with the statutes of state and federal law as it pertains to the Winter Celebration being performed here at . . ." He checked his notes. "Excuse me, um—Hartville? Is that where I am? Oh yes, here it is. Hartville Elementary.

"We are also serving you and the city with legal notices regarding this infringement of rights by our clients, which I would say is the view represented by the majority of those in attendance tonight [APPLAUSE], so that we have the opportunity for free speech rights in our songs, in the erection of a crèche on public property and to have open discourse in the public square."

Hewitt Lawrence III pulled a letter from his pocket and held it in his hand. It was only a business-sized envelope, but he wielded it like a machete.

"For too long people of faith have been silent about their rights, and I am here to say those days are over. I've argued thirteen cases before the Supreme Court, and our firm has filed countless friend-of-the-court briefs in cases that concern religious liberty. I want the people of Hartville to know that I will personally fight this all the way to those hallowed chambers again if I have to, but I would plead with the school board tonight, and I'll put it before the City Council as well: Stop barring the good people of this town from exercising what the Constitution freely gives.

" 'Congress shall make no law respecting an establishment of religion or prohibiting the free exercise thereof.' That's what's at stake here. The framers of that document, Jefferson and Madison particularly, wrote about a wall of separation between church and state. But the wall exists not to protect the government from people who want to talk about Jesus, but to protect the church from the greedy fingers of federal rulers."

The applause crescendoed, and Hewitt Lawrence III had the good sense to end his speech on an up note. He handed the letter to Jeannette Harris, who held it like a biology-lab frog; then he quickly left the building through the "No Exit" door.

The meeting lasted till nearly 1:00 a.m., but I went back to the office at 8:30 to get my column in for the morning's final edition. I don't know whether it was the writing, the subject matter or the personalities involved, but my view of the meeting ran in several papers in the county and was picked up nationally in the "What Other Papers Are Saying" column.

That was where a New York producer saw the piece and set up what would become the most memorable media event in town history.

PHYLLIS
COMES
TO HARTVILLE

f radio made the people of Hartville sound like idiots, television showed it in living color.

On Friday of the same week, Pastor Marty Karlsen was in his study preparing. "Turning Back the Night" scripts for *Heart to Hartville.* Mildred, his long-time secretary, who prided herself on her ability to keep her pastor interruption-free, reluctantly handed him a call slip that said "Tony Rockonsini, New York." He wasn't surprised to find out the name had been badly misspelled, but he was jolted when he heard a female voice on the line.

"Teauni," as he discovered, was calling from one of about a thousand talk shows based in New York. The host, "Phyllis," wanted to come to Hartville and hold a town meeting of sorts. All the major players would be part of the story: Atheists Against Mangers, school board officials, a representative from City Hall and a strong contingent of the Christian community, headed by none other than the Reverend Karlsen.

"How do I know you're going to be fair?" Karlsen said. "How do I know you're not going to come down here and make fools of us and cut us off in the middle of our sentences?"

"I can assure you Phyllis would never permit that," Teauni said reassuringly. She seemed so nice and genuine and understanding. "Phyllis is a very religious person herself and wants to let you tell your story as a microcosm of all the conflict there is in society about freedom of speech and religious issues."

Teauni was quite compelling, quite persuasive. By the time Karlsen hung up, he felt Phyllis was doing the congregation a great favor by allowing it to host her nationwide broadcast in Hartville Community Church. Besides, the pastor believed it was time "for the Lord to have his say in these matters."

As it turned out, Karlsen had no reason to gloat about being the first one contacted by Teauni. Simultaneously other producers and assistant producers and assistants to the assistant producers were calling every possible contact in Hartville, filling out personality sheets and rating from 1 to 5 such things as "strength of voice," "communicates well" and "grasps issues."

By the time the calls were made, just about everyone in Hartville believed they were going to be the priority guest for the broadcast. The mayor called his wife. Deacon Wright called a special staff prayer meeting at the hardware store. Dierdra Bergman Freep made a hair appointment, and D.J. Starr bought a tie. He had a total of three in his closet, but he decided he wanted something that didn't clip on.

The whole town buzzed for the next few days as satellite trucks and network syndication representatives arrived. For once the Blue Star Motel was full. Immediately following the Sunday-morning service, a technical crew started setup in the sanctuary for the Monday broadcast. The church canceled its Sunday-evening service and organized a prayer meeting outside City Hall, where the crèche would have been.

The performance of the school musical was scheduled for Wednesday, but the producers decided they had enough material with the board meeting, the City Council action and the strife over the manger. Monday morning Phyllis would arrive, and the entire country would get its first glimpse of Hartville, whether it liked it or not.

My column for the Sunday edition did not go over well. I took the last two weeks of programming on the TV talk shows and listed the subject matter for all to see.

Women who fall in love with prisoners.

People who weigh more than four hundred pounds and what they eat.

Elvis sightings. (Betty already had two tapes on order.)

Man who believes his deceased wife came back as a hamster.

Weight loss by alien abduction.

It was a pretty comprehensive list, and not the most flattering. The gist of the article was that we should not necessarily be proud to be in such company. "Town fights over a manger scene" doesn't look as good when it's aired the day before "Children who eat videotape and the parents who love them."

Most people thought I was angry at not being invited to be part of the program. The fact is, I'd gotten the same call as everyone else but decided it simply wasn't my story to tell. Sure, I wrote the column, but as I said, it was only the spark that ignited the powder keg. I was content to sit on the sidelines and observe, which is what a person in my profession is supposed to do anyway.

I could understand the motivation of the atheists. They enjoyed the press. There were so few of them that I figured they needed the publicity. When you're outnumbered and have unpopular views, you jump anytime the light of recognition shines in your corner.

In a way I could understand why the city agreed to be part of the program. In an age when public officials are derided for their lack of activity, they wanted to be seen as on-the-ball leaders, willing to tackle tough issues with a level head. Plus, exposure on national television was something no political figure could refuse.

However, I could not figure out the reaction of the church people. They could only come off looking angry on television and turn off potential converts. They would not mix their manger with Santa and would fight until the plywood Jesus was in his rightful place, alone on the lawn of City Hall. Pluralism was more offensive to them than an outright ban, so the crèche stayed on the sidewalk in front of Wright's Hardware.

From what I knew about religion, church people were supposed to be loving, kind, forgiving folks who reached out to the hurting in the world. In my mind their résumé read something like "Cross-bearing, widow-and-orphan-helping, sin-forgiving, joyful, self-denying, nonjudgmental followers of Jesus."

The Christians of Hartville must not have read the same press release, because they were anything but. I figured if there was a God, and I didn't hold out much hope, he would have to be awfully disappointed in the likes of these people.

But I did know one person who did live up to those ideals: Evelyn, my wife. Though she attended Hartville Community Church, she hadn't said much about the uproar over the column or the protests. She is one of those rare people who have a deep faith and manage not to make you feel like Attila the Hun when you don't share it.

A couple years after Brian was born, she approached me and said she had "accepted Jesus as her personal Savior." I laughed out loud and told her if she wanted to believe in fairy tales it was all right. If it made her feel better to throw her brain out the window she could do it. "Just don't try to make me believe that mush," I said, "and don't give them any of our money." After that she took the girls to church while I watched Brian with one eye and read the Sunday paper with the other.

And she didn't push church on me. I could tell she wanted me to believe, but there were too many unanswered questions for that. I was glad to have a morning of relative peace on Sundays with Brian. When he turned four she started taking him and I stayed by myself.

I'm not saying Evelyn's a saint. She can get beet-red and yell as loud as anybody. But when it came to religion, she was gentle and considerate. She didn't wear Bible-verse T-shirts or play Christian videos with hidden messages. It made me think there was something real about it, at least for her, but I never brought the subject up.

In all those years since her big change, I had never set foot in Hartville Community Church. I felt guilty and a bit awkward when Christmas and Easter rolled around and almost everyone in town slid into a pew somewhere. So it felt strange when I walked in for the first time and saw all the cameras and lights and cables and Phyllis' red hair.

The church held nearly three hundred people on the floor of the sanctuary and another two hundred in the balcony. The room was laid out in a horseshoe configuration, with railings extending from the pulpit to each wall. The pews were wooden and creaked when you sat down, but the place was comfortable. When bathed in the brightness of television, the sign at the front of the platform took on even greater meaning. It said, "You are the light of the world. A city set on a hill cannot be hidden."

Phyllis did not come out until two minutes before airtime. Before that a man named Stan coached us on how to raise our hand if we wanted to say something and how not to talk unless we had a microphone. I guess they had some problems with people not following those rules up in New York, but it seemed pretty logical to me.

The pulpit was removed, and several nice chairs were arranged in a semicircle on the platform. The church was full an hour before the broadcast, and some people scrunched up in the choir loft behind the platform. A few even stood in the empty baptistery to get a glimpse of the audience.

And what an audience it was. Every inch of pew space was filled with an atheist or a Christian or a person who'd seen Jesus in the snowdrift. The mayor was there. The City Council members were there. The school board, all of the teachers, half the parents and even the school choir: it was wall-to-wall Hartvillians.

Pastor Karlsen was enraptured as he gazed at the scene. I could see the wheels of faith spinning in his head, wondering what great things he might be prompted to say in this, the greatest opportunity for evangelism he had ever experienced.

Dierdra Bergman Freep had an equally curious look on her face. It was the first time she had been in a church since her father dragged her there while she was in her teens. She looked like an injured animal caught in a trap, ready to claw someone or chew her own leg off. Or both.

Phyllis pranced out of the pastor's study and waved as the town fawned. You don't think you're actually in awe of someone on television until you see them up close. Makeup powdered her shoulders like fresh snow on a ski slope. I figured the Christians would be the least impressed, since they had boycotted most of the sponsors of Phyllis' programs at one time or another. But when she appeared through the door there was an audible gasp from the room, and several older ladies said, "Aw, there she is," like she was a high-school pal returning for a reunion.

Phyllis now had a production company, had starred in three made-for-television movies and had more money than all of Hartville combined. She had flaming red hair that swished from side to side as she ran back and forth through the audience. She wore several prominent rings and held the microphone just right so they sparkled anytime she held it to her pouting lips.

The theme music blasted through the speakers, and everyone covered their ears except for D.J. Starr. He was smiling and fiddled with his new tie.

The morning sun reflected off the snow and through the stained-glass windows, casting a collage of brilliant colors around the sanctuary. There were poinsettia plants in every corner and huge red bows on the organ and piano at either side of the platform. It was quite homey, I thought, just what Phyllis would want. Like coming home to see relatives, except the relatives were about to kill each other.

I was not allowed to use a transcript of the program for this book. I guess it's one thing to deal with D.J. and Hartville Radio and another to deal with New York. Anyway, as a journalist I do cultivate a rather strong memory, particularly of things like train wrecks, plane crashes and live television programs.

Phyllis welcomed her viewers to beautiful Hartville, looking into the camera one moment and down at her notes the next. She did not use a TelePrompTer but bobbed her head down toward her hand, then up toward the camera as she introduced each guest. She described Hartville as a quaint town with modest vital statistics: a small population, abundant churches and a low crime rate. A videotape inset of the town square rolled on the video monitors, and Phyllis said, "This is the main point of contention in Hartville, because right in the spot you're seeing in the town square, a fifty-year-old tradition has come to an end. And it is mainly because of this woman that you no longer see Mary and Joseph and the baby Jesus lying in the manger."

The monitors quickly cut from the video to a tight shot of the villain. "Her name is Dierdra Bergman Frip," Phyllis said, straining to see her notes. "Is it Frip or Freep?"

"Freep," Dierdra said.

"Freep—I'm sorry," Phyllis said.

There was a tiny ripple of laughter mixed with hisses from the audience, though about a dozen from Atheists Against Mangers began to hoot and clap.

"Why, Dierdra?" Phyllis said, putting her hand behind her head, her neck disappearing. "What's so wrong with a few biblical figurines? Come on, it's Christmas."

Dierdra leaned back like she was about to spit into the wind, then shot forward and released her first volley.

"First of all, I resent having to appear in this place, which is anything but a neutral site," she snarled. Her eyebrows were raised like an angry piano teacher ready to bring the lid down on a student's fingers.

"Secondly, this country has no right to support a religion, be it Christianity or Islam or Buddhism or anything else. The people who began this country came here to get away from state-sponsored religion, and most of the people you see here today want to oppress us with their fundamentalist, Bible-thumping beliefs. They want to shove their morality and their God down our throats, with their plywood Jesus and their small-town Christianity, and we won't stand for it. This country is too great to be taken over by the likes of them."

"Reverend Marty Karlsen is the pastor of Hartville Community Church," Phyllis said quickly. "Reverend, you've been in the middle of things from the start. What's this all about?"

More than anyone on the panel, Karlsen should have felt at home, but a sudden look of fright, almost terror, came over him. His face turned pale and his lower lip quivered slightly as he cleared his throat. I heard someone in the cameraman's headphones say, "Mark an edit." Some areas of the country would see a tighter taped version of our town meeting.

"Phyllis," Karlsen finally said, "what we have here is an age-old battle between good and evil. Between truth and error."

The more he spoke, the more comfortable Karlsen became. An "amen" behind me gave him confidence as he picked up the cadence.

"It's a battle between light and dark. You know, darkness cannot stand the light."

"No," Dierdra interrupted, "we just can't stand your bullying."

"Let him talk," an older voice shouted from the balcony.

"They gave you your turn, now let him have his," another said.

"Go ahead, Reverend," Phyllis said.

"They've actually taken the Bible off the desk of a teacher because they say it endorses religion. I feel sorry for people like Dierdra here who don't have an anchor, who don't have a moral compass for their lives."

"Oh, don't feel sorry for me, Reverend," Dierdra smirked.

"I pray for people like this to . . ."

"Don't waste your prayers on me, Reverend." Each time Dierdra said "Reverend," it sounded like a word used in a shipyard rather than inside a church.

Dierdra and the Reverend were still going at it when the saxophone music swelled and Phyllis put the microphone near her tonsils and said, "And we'll be back."

After the first break Phyllis ran around the church some more and fluffed the back of her hair. When Pastor Karlsen spoke, so did Dierdra. The folks from Atheists Against Mangers hooted, and the rest hissed and booed at them, and I wondered if Phyllis wouldn't cut to the man with the reincarnated hamster before the show was over.

At one point Phyllis, exasperated with the Christians, put one hand on her hip and said, "Reverend, if these people don't want to fa-la-la-la-la with the rest of you, why do you have to force the issue?"

There were some faces on the panel who weren't Hartvillians. I guess the people of Hartville hadn't done well enough on the tests to hold down the show by themselves, so Phyllis and crew brought in some ringers just in case. One was president of the AUSCS, Americans United for the Separation of Crèche and State. Beside her was legal counsel for CCMAD, Concerned Citizens for Manger Displays. Hewitt Lawrence III, impeccably dressed as usual, was on the end, bouncing uncomfortably on his chair. All three looked like the aluminum foil on the top of a hot tin of Jiffy Pop. If they didn't talk soon I thought they would burst and spill out on the poinsettias.

"Here's another perspective to add to the case," Phyllis said, straining to see another tiny note card. "This is Reverend Tal Errant, professor of Bible and psychology at Progressive Theological Seminary located on the West Coast, and author of *Pluralistic Christianity: Orthodox Hedonism in the Sacred Paradigm.* And you say what, sir?"

The professor was the most likable person on the panel, because he seemed to be having the most fun.

He smiled and laughed a lot and raised his eyebrows when people hooted and hissed.

He had a thin face, and I could tell his glasses were a great necessity because of their thickness. He looked distinguished but not prudish. Unlike Reverend Karlsen, he wore no tie or any hint of polyester.

"I think this whole discussion is superfluous," Errant said. "We have one side that takes a literal view of the Bible and another side that doesn't want anything to do with religion. The problem is one of inclusion. If Ms. Freep felt heard in her complaints, if her feelings were validated by the other side, she might not be so adamant about her position."

The audience sat slack-jawed, trying to figure out what the professor was saying. Phyllis squeezed her forehead with one hand and shot the microphone to her mouth. "Explain."

"Certainly. The problem with this type of religious expression in the current milieu is its exclusivity. It preaches a stiff, pharisaic gospel that says it alone has the only truth and one must believe the same in order to be in the club.

"We've found it more effective to teach a biblical inclusion for all people. In other words, we boil the Bible down to those things on which everyone agrees, and we emphasize those rather than getting stuck on whether Jesus was born of a virgin or actually raised from the dead.

"For example, we refer to the Being our good Reverend Karlsen would call 'God' as 'Our Eternal

Father/Mother' or 'the All Knowing IT.' We emphasize the aspects of the Christmas story that deal with peace, goodwill toward men—excuse me, humans—and we leave out the more offensive aspects for the incarnation-impaired.

"We even have a New Testament for atheists that I'm sure Ms. Freep would benefit from reading. We take out all references to a transcendent deity and replace them with evolutionary terms."

"Could you read a bit of it for us?" Phyllis said.

"Surely. This is the traditional Christmas story from the Gospel of Luke."

The professor poked at his glasses and held the thin book two inches from his face. He read conversationally,

And there were shepherds, male and female and of all socioeconomic strata, nearby, working the third shift with their flocks. And suddenly a shooting star or some other explainable natural phenomenon occurred, and they all had a panic attack. So one of them looked at another and said, "Let's assuage our fears by going down to Bethlehem and finding a baby. Looking at a child renews my faith in humanity."

So they hurried off, praising themselves for such a good idea, and they found Mary and Joseph and the baby, who was lying in the manger, depriving the animals of their rightful place to feed.

"You know, that's what I believe," Phyllis said happily. "I believe God is love and he doesn't care what you call him as long as you're sincere and are a good person and try really hard."

The professor smiled and nodded profusely. Pastor Karlsen tried to say something, but Dierdra interrupted and bedlam ensued. The floor director made a signal, and Phyllis held the microphone close. I strained to hear her as she lowered her voice and punched out over the clamor and music: "Maybe the crux of this town's story is that for too long we've mixed so much religion with Christmas. And we'll be back."

The rest of the program can best be described as controlled mayhem. One guest accused the Christians of being Santa-impaired. Members of the congregation stood to show T-shirts proclaiming "John 3:16," "My Boss Is a Jewish Carpenter" and "Grace Happens" slogans.

One audience member showed her business prowess by publicizing her alternative to "Santa's Workshop." She grabbed the microphone from Phyllis, but Phyllis hung on. It was a furious tug of war, and I thought they were going to get to the top of the microphone, do scissors and throw the thing in the air like a baseball bat, but Phyllis finally regained control and the lady let go.

She was owner of "Yonder Stall Portraits," a manger scene complete with life-size wise men, animals and Jesus' family. For three dollars, children could skip Santa's lap and have their picture taken beside the manger, worshiping the infant King. The audience applauded as she held up an example of her work.

Toward the end of the program the atheists made disparaging remarks about home-schoolers. The Christians brought up the Bible on the desk incident again, and the story of a local boy who was not allowed to pray silently at the lunch table. The parents wanted to sue, and the kid was upset because his pig in a blanket got cold. Another parent complained that high-schoolers were forbidden to kneel in the end zone after a touchdown. From there the credits rolled, and I honestly thought somebody was going to get killed.

When I thought about it later, I remembered that Dierdra's boys were taking in the entire scene—especially the younger one, Rob. He listened to people talk about Christmas and the manger, and for the first time I actually saw him sit still. Of course it's easy to see the beginnings of disaster when you look at it over your shoulder.

"WINTER CELEBRATION"

here wasn't much of a "Winter Celebration" at Hartville Elementary School that year. The Christians pulled their kids out of the performance and threatened to never let them come back, vouchers or no vouchers. A couple hundred of them gathered in front of City Hall without the manger. There, led by Deacon Wright, they bellowed out without reserve all the carols that spoke of Jesus, the Lord and the angelic host. There just wasn't anyone there to hear them.

At the school the show went on, but something was missing. A boycott by half the town is tough on third-graders. The teachers were caught in the middle. The administration tsk-tsked and predicted it would all blow over, but it didn't. At least not in time for the performance.

At the concert Frosty had lost most of his "thumpety-thump-thump." Rudolph didn't have his usual zing either. When the kids sang, "Oh you'd better watch out," there was a distinct feeling that we really should. But who should we watch out for, Santa? The church folks? God?

When the program arrived at the humming of "Silent Night," there was an eeriness about the place. You could almost reach out and break the tension like an icicle hanging from the eaves. It seemed to me both groups in Hartville were missing something. Like we'd look back on the end of the year with deep regret.

Until that night the strife in Hartville had not been personal for me. Like any trained professional, I could view the column and resulting recognition it afforded as another person watching from the wings. As I look back, it was like my fathering. I didn't have to participate. I could view it as just another occurrence at my station in life and switch to another channel.

Watching the children on stage, engulfed in the darkness and innocence of childhood, sparked a glimmer of feeling in me. Their faces, so many mouths making such little noise, reached a forgotten part of my soul.

I took a mental journey of Christmas musicals that night. How many times had I sung "Jingle

Bells," how many times had parents been encouraged to jangle their keys? No matter how small the part, the fear and anxiety were overwhelming. How I feared making a fool of myself in front of all those kids and all those parents. My parents. I was afraid to sing out in fear I would be off-key, and I was afraid to sing quietly in fear of the director's stern looks. I dreamed I would somehow bring disgrace on our family and forever be listed in the gossip hall of shame in our town. I went over all the possibilities of failure: tripping on the stairs, falling off the risers, forgetting my pants.

Everything came back, including my fervent prayers to a silent God.

"If only you'll get me through this one night," I pleaded, "if only you'll help me remember these lines. Oh God, please, please help me not to screw this up. Please don't let them laugh at me. I just don't want to be the jerk this year."

And I would bargain with God, things like all my allowance for the next year or a vow to attend church every Sunday and memorize verses and be kind to my siblings and obey everything my mom and dad said. The promises kept mounting with the intensity of the fear.

But no matter how hard I prayed or how much I promised, I couldn't get over the feeling that the Almighty was really ticked off at me. "How many times have you asked this?" I could see him looking over the portals of heaven, like the wizard's face as

Dorothy approached. "You sniveling little wretch of a boy, I'll show you!" (Cue thunderbolt.)

Each year something happened. I would forget a word or a phrase or feel I was going to get sick and run off stage or rip my costume or sing through a humiliating quarter rest.

I was a small kid. The few surviving pictures of my youth are scattered images of missing teeth and a broken arm and leg and an occasional gash above an eye. I was clumsy. Awkward. And each year the director strategically placed me on the risers so that my tripping or loss of balance had a cruel domino effect on the rest of the group. And the parents would laugh, and the director would put his hand over his face and shake his head, and the kids would secretly wish me to the art club.

The human derision felt painful, but the crushing blow was the laughter of God. Even as a child I felt his holy "gotcha." Each year I grew further and further from God until I put him away with the rest of Christmas legends, fairy tales and hopes that went unfulfilled. If there was a God, I thought, he was either wholly impotent or massively cruel to the likes of me. This was my conclusion after only a few years of life, and I hadn't even considered global suffering.

A thousand pictures flashed through my mind as I watched those kids sing. I remembered my anticipation of the Rudolph special on television. The first year it came on there was unbridled fascination

with Clarice and Yukon Cornelius and Hermy who
wanted to be a dentist. I was thrilled with the
Abominable Snowman and a bit puzzled by the dys-
functional Santa whose wife constantly stuffed him
and criticized his lack of weight gain.

Television bound our family together at
Christmas. A ball of light glowed in every
Hartvillian window as the Grinch made his way
down to Whoville with his dog Max. Down to the
houses where all the men looked like C. Everett
Koop.

I thought about Charlie Brown's Christmas tree.
The voices of those kids in that first Christmas special were perfect, could never be matched again.
Little Linus with his nasal voice, wrapped in a blanket as a shepherd, told Charlie Brown he wasn't a
blockhead for choosing the ugliest tree. I suppose
the feeling I got from that cartoon has stuck with me
my entire life.

The images of childhood sometimes yield tradition, so on Christmas Eve I gather the kids and we
sit in front of the television with a fresh tub of popcorn. The kids are dressed in pajamas, their hair
still wet from the bath. The scent of unrinsed baby
shampoo fills the air. We sit together as a family and
watch one of these old programs. One year it's the
Grinch. The next we pull out Alistair Sim's por-
trayal of Ebenezer Scrooge. We share the transformation each story brings, whether it's the voice of
Boris Karloff or Jimmy Stewart playing George

Bailey or old Ebenezer. We share the warmth and love of Bob Cratchit for Tiny Tim.

And then the year came back, locked away in a forgotten part of my soul. The year I wept. As the Ghost of Christmas Future showed Scrooge the shadows of things that were to come, I wept. These were shadows that had already materialized in our own lives.

I watched my two daughters in the gymnasium of Hartville Elementary performing safe songs in a politically correct culture, and I felt the shoe of my son Brian slapping against my leg, then banging on the folding chair. Back and forth, back and forth, thud, bang, thud, bang. My Brian, such a wounded little Tim.

Seven years earlier we had rejoiced over the news of twins soon to be born. Lily and Kelly bubbled with excitement, and Evelyn was nesting for two, cleaning and rinsing everything she could find. I think she even washed the dirt in the back yard. The preparations were like Christmas. We cleared the spare room and bought two cribs. I splattered the walls with sky-blue Dutch Boy and allowed Evelyn to stencil a border of pink bears on parade. We would be a large family, something Evelyn had dreamed about, and I would have a son. At least I thought the odds were pretty good.

During the early stages of labor, something went wrong. I was ushered out of the delivery room, and Brian was taken quickly to surgery. Brian's tiny sister—I could have held her in the palm of one hand—never took a breath of air. We named her Rachel, a little lamb never warmed by her mother's love.

Brian was stronger and struggled from his mother's womb. But when the doctor came to me, his mask pulled from his face like a dirty napkin, I could tell my little boy would need more than a crutch and a rich benefactor whose priorities had changed.

Perhaps Brian's brain damage was more difficult for me to face than his physical problems. I wanted to teach my son baseball and football. I wanted to share stories and pocketknives and his first glove. But that day I held a broken son, a damaged life. It was terrible thinking I would never coach his Little League team, but it was the thought that I would never be able to break through into Brian's world that crushed me. Words were my life. I put them on paper and sent them into the world. I scattered words the way a farmer scatters seeds in a field. But I would not share many words with Brian, and I could not enter his dull world of sight and sound.

There were numerous surgeries. Evelyn worked with him each day, and eventually he learned to walk and could actually run with a shuffling motion. We found ways to communicate. We understood thirst. We knew his sign of hunger and fatigue. But there was no communication on any deeper level, nothing more than a word or two, and I knew the same "gotcha" had struck again in my life. The domino had tumbled onto our family, this time with lasting effects. I would not look at my son for seven years without thinking of the cruelty of God. In those years, I never saw Brian without thinking of God's anger toward me and the human race.

I tasted Christmas that night at the Winter Celebration. I tasted all my Christmases as if they were rolled into a huge ball of snow and thrown at me by a mean-spirited deity. I turned in time to get hit full in the face. I tasted Christmas through my children again, watching them sing and dance pathetically, seeing myself again and not able to turn away. I saw each of us as a Cratchit or a Tim or an empty chair, only this was not a story from long ago. It was life. It was now.

My breath floated before me in the cold like Christmas memories, and we drove home silently with our children. Outside, houses brightly dotted the landscape with their decorations. The smell of little chocolates, mints and striped candy canes rose from the back seat.

"You guys were good tonight," I said.

Nothing came but the sound of little mouths busy with candy.

"You sure were," Evelyn said. "We were both real proud of you."

Chew, chew, suck, crackle . . . crunch.

"Brian, don't bite the candy cane, bud," I said. "You're supposed to just hold it in your mouth."

Crunch, crunch, crunch, crunch.

THE
CHRISTMAS EVE
CRISIS

orld War I came to a halt one Christmas. The story says soldiers in the midst of furious battles laid down their arms for a day of peace. They ate their meager rations together and exchanged small gifts.

It was not so in Hartville. The verbal Scud missiles continued. Someone hung two angels from the cedars at City Hall. They were taken down the next day and in their place was a note that said, "Unapproved expression of sentiment toward religious holidays is strictly forbidden."

People settled into the Yuletide routine, but the animosity was thick. You could have measured it by the pound as Christians passed the town square. By Christmas weekend it was clear that Hewitt

Lawrence III had failed the faithful. In a conversation with Pastor Karlsen, the lawyer expressed deep regret that there were other cases that would take him to the Supreme Court faster and he was going to concentrate on them. Perhaps that was when the change in Karlsen began.

The weather turned colder, and grown children came to town to spend the holidays with their families. The people of Hartville enjoyed food and friends and did their best to put the conflict behind them.

On the Friday before Christmas a group from the Community Church moved the crèche from the front of Wright's Hardware to Hartville Park on Grace Avenue. They were having trouble getting the wise men to stay in a standing position and were forced to lean them against parking meters, which was a violation of a city ordinance against foot traffic impedance. The whole scene was soon loaded onto the back of a pickup and given a police escort to the second-base area of the softball field in the little park. It was not a happy day for the Christians, but they conceded that the crèche was becoming a hazard on Main Street, what with all the honking and people stepping over the fallen wise men.

Christmas Eve fell on a Sunday that year, and Evelyn took the girls to the church's candlelight service. I stayed with Brian and watched *It's a Wonderful Life*. We planned to play a shorter video when the girls returned, but as it turned out, we didn't watch anything together that year.

Evelyn turned as they were leaving. "You know you're welcome to come with. You're always welcome."

I nodded and folded my arms, my navy-blue sweater bunching underneath. "I'll stay with him," I said. "It's safer here tonight, I think."

Evelyn liked taking Brian with her. The girls loved to see him dressed up, and families at the church made a general fuss over his presence. But I was using Brian that year, as I had done when he was younger, to escape even the possibility of attending a service.

I *was* curious about the pastor's message. He had come by the office early Saturday while I finished a column and tidied my desk. He looked subdued, almost contrite, as he shuffled across the Elvis throw rug in Betty's office and came to my door to shake my hand.

"We'd love to see you at the service tomorrow night, Jack. I think you'd find it quite interesting. Maybe even get another column out of it."

"I appreciate that, Pastor, but the last time I came, I didn't know if I'd make it out in one piece. Is there a wrestling match this year, or the same old hymns and a sermon?"

"No." Karlsen smiled. "It's an intriguing idea though. I'll have to give the wrestling match some thought."

Karlsen turned serious, his brow inching closer to his eyes.

"Evelyn will be there with the girls, I suppose."

"I suppose."

"I hope you never take her for granted, Jack."

He said it in such a preachy tone, like I had never considered what a wife I had. But he *was* a preacher, so I bit my lip and tried to smile.

"Well," Karlsen said, "we would love to have you. It's going to be a service the whole town won't forget."

I couldn't stand one more thing I couldn't forget, so I opted for Jimmy Stewart and Donna Reed, a pleasant memory. I actually had never seen *It's a Wonderful Life* until the weekend after our wedding. Evelyn had insisted we watch it together by candlelight. I can still remember that little black-and-white television with the rabbit ears. In those days the movie was on every station in half-hour increments, so we picked the one with the clearest reception and settled under the covers, a candle flickering on top of the television. For this reason that film has taken on special meaning through the years.

I sat Brian in his chair by the hearth. A fire was crackling, and the wood smoke smelled heavenly. Like a scratch-and-sniff Norman Rockwell. Brian liked to sit and watch the embers glow. Every now and then he put his hand out to feel the heat and then smiled.

I turned on the VCR and he watched, his head swaying back and forth like a doll's. I wondered what was going on in his mind. Did he know anything about me other than the word *Dada?* Could he comprehend the change of seasons and the reason there was a tree in our living room with brightly wrapped presents underneath? He could say individual words and even associate them correctly. *TV* was a favorite—upon hearing it he generally rushed down the stairs to the family room. He knew *dinner* and *lunch* and *Jesus,* which came out "deenuw" and "lutch" and "Deesus."

"This is one of my favorite movies of all time," I said to him gently. I talked this way often when we were alone, his head swaying to my voice. "It's the story of George Bailey and all the people who were changed by his life. He didn't understand what a difference he had made."

Brian seemed to perk up at different points in the film. When the children went shovel sledding, he cooed and put a hand to his mouth. When the high-school dance led to the swimming-pool scene, he seemed to laugh, his mouth open wide and an "ahhhhh" sound coming forth.

I saw a look of connection in his face—then, realizing he needed a change of diaper, I felt foolish. Every parent of a disabled child has the same hope. You dream of a breakthrough experience like Helen Keller's with the water. I held hope that Brian would suddenly scratch a word in the sandbox and let us know he understood everything we said and did for him. But that day hadn't come and never would, I thought.

I changed him and sat down with a cup of coffee. George was at the prayer scene, pleading with God to show him the way. Clarence would be along soon as an answer to that prayer, and I thought about all the times my feeble petitions had fallen on deaf ears.

Voices outside stirred me from my chair, and I went to the front window. Our home is not far from Main Street and only a couple of blocks from the church. Evelyn and the girls had walked there, but it was much too early for them to be back.

I opened the drapes and beheld an amazing sight. A stream of candles poured down the church steps onto the sidewalk—all the little yellow lights running to and fro, then extinguished by the biting wind. There was a knock at the door, and I glanced at Brian before answering it. He was looking at the fireplace again, his hand stretched toward the warmth.

"Jack, you're not going to believe it," Betty Stanton said as I opened the door. A cold blast shot through the entry and my sweater too. "You're just not going to believe it."

"Come on inside, Betty."

"There's no time. I've got to get back right away and help."

"Help who? What's going on?"

"It happened at the church."

"*You* went to church?" I said in disbelief.

"I went because of the pastor," she frowned. "He came to the office yesterday and said he was going to make an announcement tonight about the manger wars."

"So it was a working religious experience." I laughed.

"This is serious, Jack. Dierdra Freep's kid is missing."

My mouth dropped. "Which one?"

"The little one that bounces off everything. Rob, I think."

"Yeah, Rob's the younger one."

"The pastor had just started his speech or sermon or—oh, whatever you call it—and Dierdra came running inside. Everything stopped, I mean everything. You could have heard a Communion wafer drop. She was sobbing and said the little fellow had disappeared twenty minutes earlier. The front door was open and his coat was gone."

"And that's where everyone's going, to look for him?"

"Except your wife. She sat Dierdra down to warm her up with some coffee. The poor thing was out in the weather with only a sweater. Didn't even take time to get her own coat."

I looked back at Brian, who was still by the fire, swaying aimlessly like a toy horse.

"I'm headed out with the rest to look," Betty said. "We could sure use your help."

"I'd like to, but I have Brian with me," I said, but Betty was already chugging down the steps toward Main Street. I could see her breath puffing like smoke from a steam locomotive. It would mean serious work on the sidewalk if she fell.

I ran my fingers through my hair and cursed. Something in me wanted to be the hero and find the boy, but with Brian it seemed impossible. I went downstairs and turned off the television.

"Hey buddy, you want to go for a walk with me?"

Brian stared at the fire.

"Outside?" I said.

He turned, and the look on his face showed he understood. Brian loved anything outside. "Outside" meant playing in dirt and eating it and sitting in sand. He shot past me in a shuffle, heading toward the closet. Dressing Brian for winter weather is as easy as putting socks on a walrus. But this night he watched quietly as I zipped his snowsuit and pulled his hat over his ears. I stood him up, and his arms stuck out from his body. He looked just like any other kid going out to play.

Unfortunately, I couldn't find Brian's shoes; this dilemma was not uncommon, but presented a great problem in this particular situation. I looked by the fireplace, then flew into the closet in a frenzy, but came up empty. Then I remembered seeing house shoes for Brian and the girls in Evelyn's closet. They were wrapped and under the tree, and I opened two packages before I found his. They were fluffy, foamy shoes called Snugglers, made by the Snuggle Slipper Factory.

"New shoes," I said, jamming them on his feet, the wrapping paper all around us. They looked comfortable but wouldn't last a minute in the snow. I threw on my coat and put Brian on my shoulder.

The night was blue. Stars sprinkled the sky, and the moon was already high above us. It made stick shadows of the trees against the snow. I could hear voices yelling as I turned toward the church. Others were moving down Main Street, so I headed west along Grace.

Brian put his face next to mine. I could feel his breath against my neck, warm and soft. Every few steps he sniffed, and the sniffing was getting wetter and wetter. I pulled a handkerchief from my pocket and wiped his nose. I told him to blow, but he did not understand.

We turned down Grace and came near the manger scene, now deserted. Gaudy Christmas lights, blue, red and white, surrounded the lean-to and cast a department-store shine on the scene. If you looked at the crèche from just the right angle and from enough distance, you might have thought the construction quaint and sturdy. But from the side you could see that Mary, Joseph and the three wise men were simply plywood cutouts. Whoever had painted them did not grasp the form of the human face. The eyes were too close on Joseph, too far apart on Mary. The gift of gold came in bars like you would see in

Fort Knox. The other two wise men held weird-looking boxes. I thought it a gift the artist had not attempted to render frankincense and myrrh.

The manger was crudely built, which actually was refreshingly realistic. It was simply an animal trough with hay brimming over the sides. The animals had been donated by Henderson's World of Ceramics on the edge of town, so there was an abundance of geese, deer and even a flamingo, but only one tired-looking sheep and a pig with a rather smarmy look on his face. This was a Hartville manger. This was what all the fuss was about.

We were half a block away and heading toward Maple when Brian spied the sight and grabbed my neck. "Main-nuw," he said, trying to say *manger.* "Main-nuw."

If Brian had been walking, I would have been able to give a few sharp tugs on his hand to bring him along. I probably would have put myself between him and the lighted scene to our left and shielded him, but because he was wearing his Snugglers and in my arms, he came, he saw, he wiggled. Veni, vidi, viggli.

"We can't see the manger right now, bud. There's a little boy out in the cold, and we need to find him."

"Main-nuw," he said, a little louder.

I wiped his nose again and continued toward Maple. If little Rob was hiding in his mother's basement, I would kill him, I thought.

"Main-nuw!" Brian screamed. My son is not a vocal child, but when he wants something there is very little that will stop him.

"We *can't* go to the manger, Brian. *We can't.* DO YOU UNDERSTAND? *NO.* I SAID NO!"

His nose was dripping again, and I wiped it dry. I couldn't remember yelling at him that way, and something inside felt crushed that I had.

"Main-nuw," he said softly.

I knelt down and held him on my knee. He was smaller than most seven-year-olds, but still a bundle to carry. I pushed a tear across his red cheek. We had been outside only a few minutes, but already the cold was taking its toll. I had no gloves, and my hands stung as if pine needles were being pushed into them. I wondered what kind of condition Rob Freep would be in if he truly was out in the weather.

"Buddy, I can't make you understand this, but Daddy has something really important to do. We can't go to the manger."

For the longest time he looked back at me, straight in the eye, no swaying. Then he said again softly, "Main-nuw."

I picked him up and moved past a huge oak tree, toward the first house that would block the manger from our view.

"When we get back home we'll make some hot chocolate and have a snack," I said. Then I said the word *snack* again a little louder, as a mantra of good behavior. "Snack. Snack. *Snack.*"

"Main-nuw."

I did not want Brian to win this battle, for I knew the war was fought on beachheads like this one. If I stood firm during these small skirmishes, I would eventually win the war. But I felt so bad about yelling at him that I finally turned around and hurried toward the crèche.

"We're going to freeze to death anyway," I said. "Might as well enjoy the view.

"Look, buddy," I continued, "we can't stay at the manger." I knew he would cry harder when we had to leave. That's the thing about giving in: you retreat one step and the enemy grabs another hill. "We'll look at it for a minute and then we have to go, okay? Understand, bud?"

"Main-nuw," he said.

Clumps of snow fell from the trees as we walked into the open field where the blinking manger lay. The cold stung my eyes until they watered, and the scene blurred. I chuckled to myself as I thought this would be the closest I would come to a church on Christmas Eve. I would worship at a plywood Jesus with a broken little boy who had no idea what he was seeing.

We were a few yards away when I saw something in the manger. I shook my head and squinted. Was it an animal in there? No, it looked like clothing of some sort. A body.

"Main-nuw," Brian said.

"What in the world?" I said.

I heard my feet crunch through the snow. Second base was lower than the rest of the field, and the snow had blown deep. I felt it go over the tops of my shoes and sting my legs above the sock line.

The manger was a long, deep trough, and you could not see fully inside until you came close to the edge. There was Mary, looking in two directions at the same time. Joseph stood beside her with a bewildered visage. One wise man held a gold brick.

A mist rose from my mouth as I panted, the extra weight of Brian taking my breath. Together we peered over the edge of the manger, and I saw shoes and jeans and a coat and the frosted face of Rob Freep. His eyes were closed tight, and his hands looked blue in the moonlight.

I did not want Brian to see him. The sight of death might disease his already damaged mind. But before I could turn away, Brian spoke.

"Deesus," he said excitedly. "Deesus!"

I can't explain the feeling at that moment of seeing the body of that little child so still and lifeless. If he had been sacrificed in some pagan ritual it would not have been more terrifying.

But when Brian spoke, the frozen child blinked. Then Rob miraculously opened his eyes and sat up amidst the straw. He put both hands on the manger's edge and looked curiously at us.

"Are you okay?" I said, shivering.

"Who are you?" Rob said.

"We heard you were lost and came to look for you. Everybody's looking for you."

His eyes darted from one face to the other, then around the manger scene. It was as if he had fallen asleep and we were trespassers in his bedroom, though someone had definitely turned down the heat.

"Why are you out here?" I said.

Rob thrust out his chin and looked up at me. He still had both hands on the manger. Straw hung from the arms of his coat.

"I wanted to see."

"See what?"

"See what it's like to be Jesus," he said.

There was an uncomfortable pause as I processed his words. Did he mean he wanted more information about the real Jesus, the one his mother was so adamantly against? Or did he just want to see what lying in a cow stall was like in the middle of winter?

"Well," I said after a few moments, "how does it feel?"

Rob blew into his little cupped hands and rubbed them together. "It feels pretty cold," he said.

"Do you want to go home?"

"Yes sir."

I helped him up out of the manger and saw the plywood Jesus underneath. Rob brushed the hay from the wooden baby's face.

"Do you think you can walk?" I said.

"Yeah, I got here okay, I can walk back."

"How long have you been out here?"

"I don't know."

We struggled back through the deep snow, the wind beating our faces, taking our breath away. It had been there throughout our walk, but I had not realized it until I turned toward home. Brian hadn't said anything since he had seen the live boy step out of the manger. He looked over my shoulder at the bright scene receding. "Main-nuw," he said softly. "Main-nuw."

This was not a plea but recognition, I thought. There was something important my son had seen that everyone else had missed. Someone once said that if I knew everything going on in the mind of my child I might be astounded, but no one had ever mentioned the things going on in his heart.

Compared to Brian physically, I am an Olympic athlete. But deep under all my layers of opinion and sarcasm, underneath all the years of trying not to feel, there is a cold heart. A dead heart. Compared with my child, my low-quality-of-life son who looks at a manger with wonder, I am among the walking dead, and I realized it that Christmas Eve. I saw a dilapidated display fashioned from cheap wood and covered with snow. He saw beyond them to God made flesh, the infant King.

I held Rob's hand and squeezed Brian tightly to my shoulder until we came to my house. I had forgotten to lock the front door, and it stood open, the light from inside spilling out on the porch. The motion-sensor light above the garage clicked on as we started up the steps, and someone rushed through the living room. Evelyn opened the storm door anxiously.

"Jack, Dierdra's son is missing and everyone's out looking . . ."

Her voice trailed off as I glanced down at him, his hand high in the air clutching mine. "Oh dear God," she said and grabbed him in her arms. "Thank you, Jesus."

"Dierdra!" she yelled as she ran to the kitchen.

I saw Dierdra Bergman Freep round the corner, a paper towel twisted in a knot around her hand. In a crisis people will use the strangest things for comfort. Dierdra looked as if someone had kicked her in the stomach, but when she saw Rob, her mouth dropped open, and for the first time I saw her break into a regular, human smile. She grabbed the kid and held him so tight I thought his head would pop off.

Evelyn cried, and Lily and Kelly jumped around the room. Brian even picked up on the feeling and started to "ahhhhhhh."

I felt something on my cheek and reached to wipe it away. I caught myself before I touched it and consciously let it slide down the length of my face. It left a streak of water that came close to the corner of my mouth but then turned slightly and hung on the edge of my chin. I felt it drop and heard the slight tick as it hit and skidded down the polyester surface of my coat. It was my first act of defiance of my former life. The first moment of conscious feeling—not the crying, but letting that tear descend and fall wherever it pleased.

The women took Rob and Brian to the fireplace and wrapped them with blankets and hot-water bottles. I stood in the entry of our home, feeling for the first time. Sensing things I had long believed were impossible.

Betty ran up the stairs behind me and nearly knocked me over. "Is he here?" she panted.

"He's here, Betty."

I told her where we had found him, and she talked with Dierdra a few moments. Then she called the police and the church—something I had forgotten to do. She trudged back to the front door then, as if her mission were not yet complete.

"You did real good tonight, Jack," she said.

"Real well," I corrected, smiling.

"Funny," she snapped, and then with a sigh said, "I'm headed back to the office. Everybody's going to want to read about this tomorrow."

"Betty, it's Christmas Eve. Those papers were printed an hour ago."

"I know. Maybe I'll have them run it again. Or maybe we can put out an extra cover page or print up a single sheet and stuff it in. I don't know, we just need to tell them about tonight."

"Can't it wait until Tuesday?" I said. "It'll still be news Tuesday, won't it?"

"No, everybody will want to know what happened. And besides, the pastor says he's holding a special Christmas service for the whole town. Jack, what he started to say before Dierdra came in . . ."

Betty had a strange look on her face. There was something stirring in her as well.

"What? What did he say?"

"I suggest you show up tomorrow and find out for yourself. I've got work to do. Good night."

THE MESSAGE

o sugarplums danced in the heads of my children that Christmas Eve. All three slept like rocks until Christmas morning. We skipped the movie because of all the excitement, but continued the tradition of Dad making pancakes for everyone as they opened their stockings at the breakfast table. As usual, I was as surprised as the kids at most of their presents, and I felt bad that Evelyn had done all the shopping. I vowed that would change in years to come.

I put a recording of Evelyn's favorite Christmas songs in the cassette player and turned it low. I protest hymns or Christian music any other day of the year but allow my family this simple pleasure on Christmas morning.

There's something about a Christmas Day that doesn't like the out of doors. Christmas Day was meant for inside, the warmth of the kitchen, the smell of the fireplace mixed with the turkey or ham, spilled pancake mix getting hard on the kitchen counter, the excitement of unwrapped packages, a mountain of wrapping paper and boxes and the squeals of happy children.

I remember my father sitting cross-legged on the couch at Christmas, my grandfather next to him, his face rough with a two-day-old beard. They stood to light their pipes and looked out the window. They talked of the weather or something going on in government, and the tobacco smoke swirled around them like memories that float in the mind and saturate every part of you. That was the last Christmas we would have with my grandfather. I've carried that picture in my head each Christmas since, and I swear I can still smell the Sir Walter Raleigh.

I stood at our window holding a huge piece of fudge, much too health-conscious for a pipe. The day was white, and every now and then a car passed filled with children and presents and parents fighting in the front seat. They were obviously arguing because one of them believed there was something about Christmas that didn't like to be in a car driving to a relative's house.

I looked out at the lawn through the icicles that hung from the eaves and felt an overwhelming sense of loss, as if I had wasted so many years with anger at God and complacency toward my family. I had tried hard to become a professional and set goals and reach for stars, but when I made it to my stars they were pale in comparison with what I now felt was important.

I counted thirty-nine icicles hanging from the eaves, the same number as my own age. Thirty-nine long, impressive cylinders of nothing but water. Drips from a dirty trough. If I had taken my hand and run it across them, breaking them off at the base, I would have no more wasted them than I had my own life.

It is a very sad thing when a man finds, in the middle of his existence, that he has no real life at all. But sadder still is the one who discovers it and does not change.

The service was scheduled for 11:00 that morning. It was a strategic move on Pastor Karlsen's part, allowing enough time for the kids to open presents and get sufficiently bored with the loot. He knew all the cooks in the congregation had their roasts in by 10:00 a.m. and wouldn't be taking them out until 1:00, just before the football game. The rolls were buttered and covered with foil, and the potatoes only had to be heated and whipped. With the excitement of the evening before, Karlsen knew that many would show up who hadn't darkened the church's door since the previous year.

Most of Hartville had read the story inserted hastily by Betty. I counted three spelling errors and a couple of run-on sentences, but otherwise she had done a good job of conveying the urgency of the story. I came out looking a little less than a knight in shining armor and could only imagine what Phyllis would have done with the unfolding drama. What the town didn't know was the identity of the real hero: my son, Brian. It felt good to turn those words over in my mind. *My son.*

The church was absolutely packed. Betty Stanton would have had to lose fifty pounds to wedge one other Hartvillian into the Community Church. And it wasn't just church attenders who were there. It was people from the town who had been on the sidelines of the debate, unwilling to take sides. It was people who wore Christian T-shirts sitting next to atheists who couldn't stand the thought of the crèche on public ground. They were all people who had worked together the night before to find a little boy lost in the cold, and what they believed about mangers and words in songs took a back seat when a life was at stake.

The only one I didn't see was Dierdra, and, well, you couldn't half blame her for not showing up, given all that had happened.

I sat with one hand in Evelyn's, an arm around Brian and both eyes on Lily and Kelly, who suddenly looked very grown-up. There were young, hormonally challenged boys all around us, and it was all I could do to not slap each one and tell them my girls weren't getting married till they were in their forties.

The cynic in me said Pastor Karlsen was going to use the opportunity to preach hellfire and brimstone. At last, with no advertising blitz, Sunday-school competition or New York talk show to shape the sermon, he had a huge crowd in his church. It was a crowd that needed salvation, as far as I could tell. And as in the days of my youth, I figured there would be a couple of songs, a sermon on John 3:16 and an altar call, complete with "Just As I Am" being sung fifty times and Pastor Karlsen saying, "We're going to sing it just one more time to give you a chance to come down to the front of the church. Don't put it off." Something like that.

To my surprise, he didn't do anything like that. The organist was playing a somber version of what I later found out was called "Let the Walls Fall Down." When it was over, a nicely dressed Deacon Wright came to the pulpit and held onto it like it was the last life raft on the *Titanic*. He looked confused, and I couldn't help thinking there was some sort of disagreement between him and the pastor over what was about to happen.

"This is a special day in Hartville," the deacon said. The sound system emitted a high-pitched squeal, and Deacon Wright cupped his hand over

299

the microphone, which only made it worse. I looked to the back of the auditorium at a teenager who was fiddling with knobs and buttons on the sound board.

"Tommy, just set it and leave it alone," Deacon Wright bellowed. The squeal went away, and Tommy's face looked like a chili pepper with rouge. "This is a special day," Wright continued, "because a little boy that was lost has been found."

"Amen," a man said in front.

"It's special because we celebrate the birth of another little boy in Bethlehem nearly two thousand years ago.

"Pastor Karlsen and I talked about this service, which was supposed to be last night, and you all know what happened last night. We talked about it Friday after our radio broadcast. And I'll admit, we've had our problems over it. But for some reason the Lord has allowed all this to happen, and I think we ought to hear our pastor out. So for those who haven't been here in a while and are nervous, we aren't going to make you sing a solo or anything. We're not passing the plate for an offering, though it pains me a bit with everybody here."

A ripple of relief disguised as laughter spread through the auditorium, and Deacon Wright smiled. I could sense people leaning forward, as if in great anticipation for what lay ahead.

There is a feeling you get in a church, one that I had not experienced since I was a kid. It's a feeling that everything is right with the world. A feeling that you can relax. I settled into the hard pew, and some part of me felt good for being there. Like I was doing my duty. I was sitting through a sermon again and could afford an extra slice of pie or stretching out before the television with no guilt. I was paying my penance by just being there, and it felt good.

Wright stepped back. The crowd hushed as Pastor Karlsen came to the pulpit.

"Thank you, Deacon Wright," Karlsen said. "We *have* had our differences over the past couple of days, because I want to begin by saying we're sorry. To every one of you that we've called names or spoken harshly against in this community, I say we're sorry. To everyone, especially the fellow who was playing Santa Claus and his elves who got banged up, we want to say we're sorry. To the teachers and the administrators and the school board and the workers at City Hall and the mayor, we want to say we're sorry."

I glanced around the platform through the stillness. An American flag stood proudly to the pastor's left, the Christian flag to his right. Every star and stripe seemed to listen.

"Sorry for what?" Karlsen continued. "I think that's what every member of this congregation is asking right now. We put our hearts and souls into getting that manger back in the public square, and we fought till the very end. So what are we sorry for? Sorry for standing up for what's right? Sorry for trying to get God back in the schools where he belongs? No. There's a time to take a stand and a way to take a stand, and I'm telling you here today, on this Christmas morning, that our cause was right.

"But Jesus said, 'Love your enemies and pray for those who persecute you,' and that's where we were wrong. We did it wrong and we're sorry.

"I wish those cameras were back here from New York. I'd look right into their little red lights and I'd tell Phyllis and the panel and the whole country that we were wrong. We're sorry."

I sat with my mouth open, unable to breathe or move. Brian swayed at my side, taking my arm with him.

"We wanted to be salt and light, my friends, but we poured our salt into an open wound, and we took a blowtorch to this town. We are told to love others because he first loved us. If we say we love God but hate others, we're fooling ourselves."

Deathly silence was interrupted by rustling and a few whispers. I turned to see the door to the narthex close and someone slip into the very last row. Pastor Karlsen looked up, then stepped back from the pulpit.

"And I want to say right now," he continued, moving down past the altar and to the first pew, speaking without the aid of a microphone, "that there's one person I am particularly glad to see here today."

Tommy was frantic in the back, but Karlsen waved him off and kept walking. Though his normal voice reminded me of Mr. Haney, his preaching voice carried to the back of the room. Every head followed him as if it was the final tie-breaking point at Wimbledon.

"I don't mean to make a spectacle here, and it's probably the last thing she would want me to do, but when I saw her come in I knew I had to make one special apology, and that is to you, Dierdra. We have talked about you at our dinner tables. We have poisoned our children by calling you names, and we've turned them against your wonderful little boys. I don't care how wrong we think you may be about the manger, or how wrong we think you are about the public schools: what we have done is not right. It is not!"

"Amen," said a hundred voices in the congregation, staggered just enough to make it sound like a thousand.

"When your little boy turned up missing last night, Dierdra, it was clear as day to me that we had missed the boat. And thank God we put aside our differences for his sake."

Karlsen shook his head and put his hand over his mouth. His back was turned to me, but I could tell a wellspring of emotion was breaking forth. He moved back toward the front of the church, his lips pinched firmly shut as if he were holding a finger in a dike.

"Preacher," a voice called from behind him. "I accept your apology. For my son, and my whole family, I accept it. And I want to thank you and everybody who helped me find him. You didn't have to, but you did."

Karlsen turned, raced back to Dierdra Bergman Freep, who was now standing, and gave her the biggest hug I have ever seen a man of the cloth give to an atheist. There were many "amens" now and a lot of sniffling and wiping of eyes.

Finally Karlsen moved back to the pulpit. He wiped his eyes and forehead, then replaced the handkerchief in his breast pocket.

"I don't have any of this written down," he said. "But I want to tell you all something. You can have the best intentions, you can have truth and God on your side, and still be wrong.

"Listen to me. We were so caught up with our constitutional rights and our legal protections under the law and our convictions about freedom of religion that we forgot about the most important thing Christmas came to bring. A relationship.

"We were so high and mighty about the manger. We fought a culture war to keep God in the center of Christmas, and we let him get out of the center of our own lives.

"Let me say this to you. We can win legal battles all the way to the Supreme Court, but if we lose a soul, everything we've done will have been in vain."

I had never seen Pastor Karlsen preach, but judging from the congregation, they hadn't seen him this exercised in a while. Deacon Wright sat with his arms folded and a slight scowl on his face. There were several black members who were now rocking back and forth harder than Brian, ready to swing a handkerchief or two. "That's right," one of them said. "You know it."

"Friends," Karlsen said, "and I'm talking to members of this congregation and others who call themselves Christians, how many of us in here are for prayer in the schools? How many of you want the Ten Commandments back on the walls of our classrooms? Go ahead, raise your hands. Put them up there high so everybody can see them."

About 95 percent of the crowd raised a hand.

"That's good. That's wonderful. Now put your hands down. We've really got a consensus here, haven't we?"

"Amen!"

"That's right."

"You know it."

"Now let me ask you another question. How many of those who just said they were for prayer in the school—how many of you prayed with your children last night before they went to bed? How many of you prayed with them at the breakfast table before they went off to school last week, or prayed with them at the dinner table, more than to thank the Almighty for the food and bless it to the nourishment of our bodies?"

Apparently either everyone thought it a rhetorical question or they had just been nailed by the pastor, because no one raised a finger.

"How many of you right now can give me more than five of the Ten Commandments? Go on, think about it. Can you name them right now?

"It's easy to hold a poster or wear a T-shirt, but it's harder to really live what you believe.

"Now I've been talking to myself here the last few minutes as much as anybody. I got caught up in the fight and got swept along like a lot of you on both sides. But the whole thing comes down to this: if we believe that the God of the universe invaded time and space for us, how far will we go to communicate his message to others? How much love will we show to people who are against us?

"The message of Christmas is this, friends. The same little baby who felt the straw in the manger felt the nails on the cross. The same baby those smelly old shepherds came to see was the very Lamb of God who came to take away our sins. And if we can sit here being forgiven by the holy God of the universe, and turn around and spit venom at the people who don't know him, then God help us. We've missed it, friends. We've missed the whole reason for Christmas."

Pastor Karlsen was sweating profusely. He loosened his tie for more air. The congregation was still now. What Karlsen said next was to me. I was convinced at the time that he had read my diary, though I've never kept one.

"I've been talking about those in the church who call themselves Christians, and I know there are some of you who don't call yourselves that. I say this a lot and I mean it: I am the biggest sinner in this room. I know more about the Bible than most here, and I get paid to study and expound the Word, and the more I read, the more I see how holy God is and how sinful I am.

"The truth is, we're all in the same boat. We are all sinful, and I know that's not a politically correct term, but it's true. He has every right to cast us away and every right to drop-kick us through the goalposts of eternal punishment. Just one sin could do that, let alone the hundred I commit every day."

"Preach it."

"You know it."

"Amen."

"But you know what? Here's the good news about Christmas. Are you listening?"

"We're listening, Lord," a voice behind me said.

"God isn't mad at you anymore," Pastor Karlsen said. *"God isn't mad at you anymore!* Do you know that? Do you believe that?"

A smile came across Karlsen's face like a golden sunrise on a spring morning. "The Father who has every right to punish you sent his Son to die for you. And that's how I know he's not mad at you, my friend."

I bent my head and thought of all the ways God had been mad at me. All the unanswered prayers, all the holy "gotchas" of my life, rolled together into a huge knot inside my heart. Could there be a chance that God was real? Did such a being care for me?

I had pictured God with folded arms, tapping foot and a look of disdain, but this man said the Father was holding out his hands ready to embrace me.

Evelyn put her hand on my shoulder.

"I wish we could have put that manger up in front of City Hall where it had been for fifty years," Karlsen said. "But more than that, I wish I would have honored Christmas in my heart. I wish I would have shown a little bit of the love and understanding God showed me when he forgave me. I wish I would have done less talking on the radio and more praying for you folks, especially the ones of you I don't see that often.

"I come before you today, and I tell you I'm sorry for the way I've acted toward you."

Pastor Karlsen went silent for a moment. He bowed his head as if in prayer. I did not know what to do. The altar seemed too far and the arms of my wife too near.

In the midst of the indecision and the incredible silence of God, I heard a noise, a whisper to my right. It was my son.

"Deesus," he whispered. "Dank-oo, Deesus."

EPILOGUE

Everything did not come up roses for Hartville. Deacon Wright was in such disagreement with Pastor Karlsen that he left the church and took a few disgruntled members with him. A month later he started his own program on the Christian station, and his most repeated phrase was "We're not selling out like some people."

Betty Stanton experienced a real change, but her zeal was not according to knowledge. She hounded the music director of the church until he relented and allowed her to sing during an offertory one Sunday.

She wore a pink jumpsuit with bubble sunglasses. She didn't have sideburns, but she did take the microphone and swing it in big loops, almost hitting Pastor Karlsen in the head.

Then she sang:

You ain't nothin' but a sinner,

Sinnin' all the time.
You ain't nothin' but a sinner,
Depraved in the mind.
You ain't never goin' to heaven till you meet a
friend of mine.

No one doubted Betty's sincerity, but the tempo, the style and the little snarl she put in the song were too much for the congregation. She told me she was working on more acceptable tunes and hoped to sing a Christian version of "Blue Christmas" at some point. We're all holding our breath.

Despite these setbacks, there continues to be a new spirit in town. The City Council set aside a special corner of the City Hall lawn for anyone who wanted to put up a display the next year. It was basically the same rule as the year before, but the people's reaction was different. With the unanimous permission of the City Council, Hartville Community Church erected a permanent plaque to commemorate that special Christmas.

On top of the five-foot-tall cement block was a bronzed manger and an inscription that read,

In commemoration of the manger that tore us apart, the child who brought us together, and the One who offers lasting forgiveness, Hartville Community Church dedicates this monument in their honor.

The day the plaque was commissioned I wrote a very personal column describing Hartville's transformation. The next day I received what looked to me like a legal notice with a return address from an out-of-state law firm. I opened the letter and read the following:

> On behalf of my client, the undersigned, we demand the plaque to be erected on government property by the group known as Hartville Community Church be denied access to said public property unless it meets the following condition. It must refrain from using the phrase "the child who brought us together" and use instead the phrase "Rob Freep, who got away."

The letter was signed, "Dierdra Bergman Freep, JK (Just Kidding)." Beside the signature was a smiley face, and underneath she had scribbled, "I guess I'll let it slide this time, Grim."

I have kept that letter in a drawer at work, and I still pull it out periodically. On the wall beside me is a framed copy of the column that started it all, signed by Phyllis, Pastor Karlsen and Dierdra Freep.

And somewhere on my desk, amidst a cluttered pile of letters and clippings, is a picture of a family—two girls who are growing up much too fast, a husband and wife who are growing together instead of apart, and the blurry photo of a swaying child in slippers.

These are reminders of the year Hartville went away with the manger. The year I finally came home.